Tourismusverband Mecklenburg-Vorpommern/
Zeitungsverlag Schwerin (eds)

JANA SPERBER

World Class

100 Anecdotes from
Mecklenburg-Western Pomerania

HINSTORFF

Dear Participants, dear Guests,

The holiday state Mecklenburg-Western Pomerania and the Hanseatic City of Rostock welcome you to the 35th Germany Travel Mart. For the first time the GTM is being held in the region which, year for year, attracts the most German summer holidaymakers. And more and more foreign guests are delighting in the beaches, culture and active holidays offered in Mecklenburg-Western Pomerania.

With your work you contribute to making Mecklenburg-Western Pomerania internationally known. This book shows how in the past Mecklenburg-Western Pomerania bridged the gap between itself and the world. Extraordinary stories tell of the links this federal state forged with many countries of the world. We would like to extend to you a heartfelt welcome to return after the GTM 2009, to discover the showplaces described in the stories and of course to enjoy the delights of this holiday state.

We wish you a pleasant stay in our state and a successful 35th Germany Travel Mart 2009 in the Hanseatic City of Rostock.

Jürgen Seidel
Minister of Economics,
Labour and Tourism of
Mecklenburg-Western
Pomerania

Sylvia Bretschneider
President of the State Parliament
and Chairwoman of the Tourism
Association of Mecklenburg-
Western Pomerania

Roland Methling
Lord Mayor of the Hanseatic
City of Rostock

Mathias Löttge
Member of the State Parliament
and Chairman of the Tourism
Association of Mecklenburg-
Western Pomerania

With friendly assistance of the European Social Fund
and the Ministerium für Wirtschaft, Arbeit und Tourismus
Mecklenburg-Vorpommern

Tourismusverband Mecklenburg-Vorpommern
(www.auf-nach-mv.de; www.linking-stories.com)
Managing director: Bernd Fischer
Zeitungsverlag Schwerin GmbH & Co. KG
(www.svz.de; www.prignitzer.de; www.nnn.de)
Chief editor: Thomas Schunck

Bibliographical information from the Deutsche Bibliothek:
The Deutsche Bibliothek lists this publication in the
Deutsche Nationalbibliographie; detailed bibliographic data
can be found on the internet at http//dnd.ddb.de

© Hinstorff Verlag GmbH, Rostock 2008
Lagerstraße 7, 18055 Rostock
Tel. 03 81 / 49 69-0
Internet: http://www.hinstorff.de

All rights reserved. No part of this publication, including
excerpts, can be reproduced, stored on computer,
disseminated through photocopies or by electronic or other
means, used in lectures, on the radio, etc. without permission
of the publisher.

First edition 2008

Production: Hinstorff Verlag GmbH
Cover design and maps: WERK 3, Rostock
Editor: Dr Florian Ostrop
Printing and binding: Westermann Druck Zwickau GmbH
Printed in Germany
ISBN 978-3-356-01264-4

Foreword	11
Maestro paints in Western-Pomerania Baltic Sea coast inspires Italian artist	12
"Lightbringer" opens window to Japan Cherry blossoms and kimonos in Mecklenburg Schweiz	14
Silver for Schwerin glass artist Medal win at World's Fair in St. Louis	15
Rügen man dug right across Sweden Millennium construction displaced Danish customs officers	17
Rostockers build library in Kenya Association enables children to go to school	19
Euro visionary in 1909 Mecklenburg chemist launched first international currency	21
Astronomer with a golden nose Tycho Brahe got his trademark in Rostock	24
Fallen hero of the skies Otto Lilienthal from Anklam laid the groundwork for modern aviation	26
Concrete with pizazz Ulrich Müther created a furore with daring roof constructions	28
Intercultural masterpiece in Güstrow European builders shaped castle architecture	30
Martha – music from Mecklenburg Teutendorf virtuoso composed in Paris and Vienna	32
Stallion in Napoleon's service White horse from Ivenack as loot in France	34
Green tea in a red pavilion A touch of chinoiserie – not far from the Baltic Sea	36
New home of the dragon boat Schwerin firm delivers all over the world	38
Underwater treasure hunt Did a Barth shipowner construct the first diving suit?	40
Tragic end off Tokyo Prussian schooner sank on diplomatic mission	41

43	**Diva at the "Karusel"**	
	Asta Nielsen relaxed at the Isle of Hiddensee	
45	**State-of-the-art at 60**	
	Rostock and Wismar send ships to the seven seas	
47	**Mecklenburg Statue of Liberty**	
	Mirow princess at the American east coast	
48	**Hanseatic soccer school in Chicago**	
	Ex-Hansa player trains youngsters in the USA	
49	**Of bockwurst and beer in Brazil**	
	South America's Pomeranian tradition	
51	**Ribnitz – scenery for comic series**	
	Feininger captured Mecklenburg and Pomerania	
54	**Warnemünders were Munch's models**	
	Norwegian captured lifeguards on canvas	
56	**Life sciences from the coast**	
	BioCon Valley part of a global network	
57	**Chalk line separates Sassnitz from Lenin**	
	Seaport was gateway to Russian revolutionaries' homeland	
60	**Relatively famous honorary doctor**	
	Rostock University dignified Albert Einstein	
62	**Pomeranian man battles his way through**	
	Max Schmeling maintains links to his birthplace	
64	**Trans-Siberian departs at Sassnitz harbour**	
	Rügen port is station of the world's longest railway line	
65	**Hairy immigrants from China**	
	Fishermen find exotic sea dwellers	
66	**Indian Sherlock Holmes from Teterow**	
	Farmer's son became commissioner of police	
68	**First white man on Easter Island**	
	Rostocker discovered Pacific island	
69	**Strelitz woman on the throne of the Empire**	
	Charlotte of Mecklenburg-Strelitz married George III	
71	**Mozart's music for Mecklenburg's monarchs**	
	Genius composed for Strelitz Dukes	

Stormy petrel on the sun island Maxim Gorky recuperates in Usedom's bracing climate	72
Looking for a homeland Writer Uwe Johnson remained devoted to Mecklenburg	74
Greifswalder surveys giant waterfall Development worker explores attraction in virgin forest	76
Wismar car in Olso museum Technical Museum houses only preserved Mecklenburg automobile	78
From the Müritz all over the seas Waren propeller manufacturer leads global market	79
Regatta network across the Baltic Baltic Sail marks the maritime summer-highlight	81
Sun King's traces in Schwerin Lake Grand Duke erected Palace following French model	82
Romanov residence near Rostock High nobility family reunion at the Baltic Sea	84
The whole alphabet on seven keys Pasewalker invents a typewriter for the blind	86
A modern surgeon Christian Theodor Billroth operated throughout the world	88
Victuals for Lord Nelson Warnemünde received important visitors	90
Mecklenburger found ancient clay tablets in Palestine Ernst Sellin excavated Jericho	91
Captivated by the Dark Continent Paul Pogge advanced from big game hunter to Africanist	92
Record-breaking oak trees in Mecklenburg Huge trees in Ivenack are among the oldest in Central Europe	94
The two sides of aerospace (Kathrin Möller) Peenemünde 1942 – rocket weapon goes into space	95
The Brockhaus plot (Frank Ruhkieck) Malchin inventor developed first petrol-powered vehicle	99
The Grande Dame of Esperanto (Frank Ruhkieck) Schwerin poet was the first to versify in the artificial language	101

103	**Neubukower bared advanced culture**	
	Heinrich Schliemann brought to light 1,000 years of Greek history	
106	**Stralsund chemist discovered oxygen**	
	Late honour for decent experimenter	
108	**Görnower saves palm trees (Frank Ruhkieck)**	
	Bioacoustics specialist Benedikt von Laar exposes a hidden pest	
112	**Wismar's Count von Count (Katharina Handy)**	
	Gottlob Frege invented the principles of programming languages	
114	**Chess Bible by Mecklenburg master**	
	Paul Rudolf von Bilguer drafted leading reference book	
116	**Swedish royal visitors in Greifswald**	
	Queen Silvia congratulates university on anniversary of its foundation	
117	**Dutchman engraved Pomeranian chronicle on copper plates**	
	Early map was extraordinary detailed	
118	**Royal landscape design in Western Pomerania**	
	Swedish queen redesigned baroque park in Löbnitz	
119	**Searching for traces in Australia**	
	Man from Rostock considered co-founder of the "Garden State" Victoria	
121	**Rostock beach-chair conquers the world**	
	Striped beach furniture delights sun-worshippers on the Pacific coast	
123	**Shopping fun from Mecklenburg-Western Pomerania**	
	Parent firm of KaDeWe located in Wismar	
125	**Ohio sings ode to Baltic Sea island**	
	Rügen song of home rediscovered in the USA	
126	**Counterpart to Chicago's Reuter statue**	
	Honour of the poet following American model	
128	**The revolutionary coupling (Peter Falow)**	
	Wismar invention initiates the great age of the railways	
131	**Orange prince from Mecklenburg-Schwerin**	
	Baltic nobility connected to Dutch dynasty	
133	**Bad Doberan attracts VIPs**	
	Europe's oldest racecourse located in Mecklenburg	
134	**Pioneer of electricity and mentor of the Tsar**	
	Rostocker won favour with Katharina II	

Western-Pomeranian know-how on the Mekong	135
Ship builder from Anklam crafts pontoon boats in Cambodia	
Rügen's chalk cliffs in Switzerland	136
Western Pomerania inspired C. D. Friedrich to produce his masterpieces	
Between Adriatic and Mare Balticum	139
Milanese painter captured Baltic Sea coast	
Mecklenburg scientist plumbs the depths	141
The sinking of the Titanic motivated the invention of sonar	
Master of the pipes	142
Wilhelm Sauer from Mecklenburg built 1,100 organs	
Baltic waves in the Dolomites	144
Declaration of love to the homeland girdles the earth	
Executioner at Spyker Castle	146
Carl Gustav Wrangel beheaded on Rügen?	
On the trail of the Tsars	148
Young daughter of the Tsar earns sympathy of Mecklenburgers	
Expedition in the Lake Plateau	149
Henry M. Doughty travelled through "Old Merry Mecklenburg"	
Japanese loves to live by the Baltic Sea	151
Satoko Kojima brings Far East atmosphere to her adopted country	
Coffee Tradition from Central America	154
Nicaraguan establishes himself with business idea	
African wild animals for European courts	156
Pomeranian taxidermist preserved for eternity	
Invitation to South Africa	158
Caspar Venter's homeland thrills Neubrandenburgers	
Estonians learn from Mecklenburg professor	159
Rostock pharmacist taught at university in Tartu	
Röntgen's teacher and trailblazer in computer technology	161
Current technology benefits from August Kundt's discoveries	
Pursuing migratory birds by bike	163
Otto Steinfatt followed migratory birds all the way to Africa	
Gateways to the world	165
International air traffic in Mecklenburg-Western Pomerania	

- 167 **Sternberg man revolutionised German shipping**
  First iron screw steamship was launched on the river Warnow

- 169 **English style seaside resort**
  International history of Heiligendamm

- 171 **Rostock family in Europe and overseas (Hans-Heinrich Schimler)**
  An emigrant story of the 19th century

- 175 **Vietnamese ambassador in Bad Doberan**
  County town exports marine technology all over the world

- 176 **Christmas parcels from Sweden**
  Jangling presents for the neighbours

- 178 **Rostock woman governed Russia**
  Anna Leopoldovna and the tsardom

- 180 **Peter I apprenticed near Lake Müritz**
  Tsar learned blacksmith's craft at castle near Röbel

- 181 **Rostock rector in Canadian gown**
  Thomas Strothotte remembered his roots at inauguration

- 182 **State funeral for Argentina explorer**
  Stralsund scholar worked in South America

- 184 **Mecklenburg's name for Maderia's souvenir**
  Keepsake owes its name to Mecklenburg-Strelitz

- 186 **Flags from the King**
  Mecklenburg dynasty in Danish service

- 188 **Artworks from Güstrow in the Far East**
  Works by Ernst Barlach exhibited in Japan

- 189 **Germany's voice in the concert of nations**
  Gunter Pleuger represented Germany at the UN

- 191 **With a wheelbarrow across Kamchatka**
  Two Rostock adventurers do extreme sports all over the world

- 193 **Silver Condor flew to the end of the world**
  Pilot with Mecklenburg roots explores Tierra del Fuego

- 197 **Honoured on the moon**
  Friedrich von Hahn's merits perpetuated in space

- 199 **Appendix**

Foreword

Dr. Gunter Pleuger

Mecklenburg-Western Pomerania and Internationality – these two concepts were inseparable in the past and will remain so in the future. This federal state in the north-east of Germany is more closely associated with the rest of the world than you might at first think. Reason enough to collate and publish some of the stories that demonstrate this fact.
Mecklenburg-Western Pomerania has produced people who have played an important role in world history. Experts in the arts and sciences developed their reputation and started their international careers on the shores of the Baltic. Theodor Billroth, a native of Rügen, for example, is regarded as one of the founding fathers of modern abdominal surgery. Emigrants from here took their homeland with them when they set sail for distant shores: even today, inhabitants of the Brazilian town of Pomerode still speak the regional dialect known as 'Plattdeutsch' or 'Low German'. Architects from here were inspired by other cultures, while international artists gained inspiration here. Again and again, people returning home brought their cosmopolitan outlook and their rich fund of knowledge to Mecklenburg-Western Pomerania. The book *World Class* contains 100 anecdotes which document the connections between Mecklenburg-Western Pomerania and the rest of the world. It shows that this small federal state has the occasional superlative to offer, and it tells the stories of unusual people and curious events. These stories were researched in the run-up to the G8 Summit in 2007, when the world's spotlight was turned on Mecklenburg-Western Pomerania as never before and the region had an unprecedented opportunity to demonstrate its excellent hospitality.

Those who have come to know and appreciate the charm of northern Germany – whether as a politician, holiday-maker, businessman or new inhabitant – cannot get enough of it. And after four decades of service in the German Foreign Office I, too, frequently return to my native land – to visit friends, refresh memories, relax and enjoy the atmosphere. This book is an ideal complement for that, and I can promise you some interesting and enjoyable hours reading it.

Maestro paints in Western-Pomerania

Baltic Sea coast inspires Italian artist

Franco Costa maintains a very special relationship with the coast. The artist works a great deal in Mecklenburg-Western Pomerania, and his work is esteemed here perhaps just as highly as in his homeland. His works of art have brought him fame and honour. Costa is a globetrotter. Born in Rome in 1934, he has travelled through China, India, Ethiopia, America; he could well be in Sweden today and Dubai tomorrow.

The artist was first enthused by the Darß Bodden (lagoon) scenery some years ago. Since then he has made many trips to the Baltic Sea spa Zingst, an inspiring place with oodles of charm. Aquatic sports have also always attracted him. The Picasso follower is a passionate yachtsman and has for a number of years been the official America's Cup artist. Furthermore, he provides artistic accompaniment to other important sailing events, including the International Regatta festival at Zingst.

With his eye for the significant, he captures fascinating moments of the sailing competition on Fischland-Darß-Zingst peninsula. The maestro completed a work for the Match Race 2005, which was subsequently presented at the International Hanseboot Exhibition in Hamburg. At the Zingst Haus des Gastes, a tourist information and restaurant, 70 paintings were exhibited right on the Baltic Sea beach front. Costa is a kind of Post-impressionist who learned from Picasso and Henri Matisse. He presents his motifs with a colourful mixture of acrylics smoothed on the canvas with a knife. The painter himself calls his art Arte Vita: life for art, and art for life.

Beside aquatics, the globetrotter also puts landscapes, towns, and nature on canvas. The piers of the three Usedom Kaiserbäder (imperial spas) and the backwater appealed to his artistic sensibilities.

Moreover, the cheerful artist is not only enthused by the Usedom evening sky and the bewitching light displays on Lake Neppermin, the old Dutch windmill in Benz touched him so deeply that he captured it on canvas.

Franco Costa has friends all around the world. His popularity does not merely derive from his artistic abilities, but rather from his commitment to helping others. He has invested in the society "Usedom Feelings", which has made sponsoring new artistic blood in the region its business.

In regard to himself, the man with the fascinating painting technique says that he wants to spread peace and serenity around the world. With this attitude, the Italian is always a welcome guest in Mecklenburg-Western Pomeranian.

Internet tip:
www.francocosta.it

Franco Costa calls his bouyant art "Arte Vita".

"Lightbringer" opens window to Japan

Cherry blossoms and kimonos in Mecklenburg Schweiz

In the middle of Mecklenburg, Mitsuko Castle is a window on Japan.

Förderverein deutsch-japanischer Freundeskreis Todendorf e.V.
Kastanienallee 21
17168 Todendorf
Tel. +49(0)39975 759797

The Japanese tea mistress Mineko floats around the room wearing a traditional kimono and serving fragrant green tea in delicate china. You could be fooled into thinking that you are in Japan. In fact, however, this ceremony is enjoyed in the heart of Mecklenburg. Mitsuko, a castle with a Mecklenburg history and a Japanese name, invites guests on a distant journey with its Far Eastern interior. Heinrich Johann Radeloff, an artist enamoured of Japanese culture, took up residence back in his homeland of Mecklenburg after a lengthy stay in Kyoto. Behind a Mecklenburg façade, he transformed the castle by erecting a Japanese centre unmatched in the entire region. Furthermore, the Ice Age scenery in the castle park will soon be transformed into a cherry tree grove.

Visitors can also savour Japanese art here. The fascinating permanent exhibition in the castle includes not only calligraphies, ceramics, art and craft work, and everyday objects from Japan but also works of the German-Japanese artist Heinrich Johann Radeloff himself.

Incidentally, the artist named his castle after his wife Mitsuko, whom he met in Kyoto. The "lightbringer" is, like the castle named after her itself, Mecklenburg's window to Japan. In the summer months, its doors are open to anyone fascinated by Japanese culture.

Silver for Schwerin glass artist

Medal win at World's Fair in St. Louis

At the St. Louis World's Fair in 1904, a glass manufacturer from Schwerin achieved remarkable success in the arts and crafts category. He won a silver medal beating rivals from Bavaria and Saxony.

At St. Louis, Rudolf Christian Carl Königsberg exhibited a leaded opal glass window with a motif depicting life in a Mecklenburg village. The United States of America had sent an invitation to the government in Berlin for the World's Fair two years earlier. The glass-maker may have heard about it via the Mecklenburg Chamber of Handicrafts. The craftsman, who was born in Crivitz on 19th September 1887, studied in America for many years. No doubt, he expanded his glass-working skills there.

From 1903 onwards, Königsberg ran his own workshop "Kunstgewerbliche Werkstatt für Glasdecoration" in Schwerin. He specialised in lead and brass glazing using American crystal and opalescent glass, which is rolled glass characterised by its marbling effect.

Königsberg must have been much in demand as a craftsman in Schwerin, too, since he also had various honours bestowed on him at home, such as the gold medal awarded to him at the regional exhibition "Allgemeine Mecklenburgische Landesausstellung". Incidentally, strolling through the capital of Mecklenburg-Western Pomerania, Königsberg's traces can still be

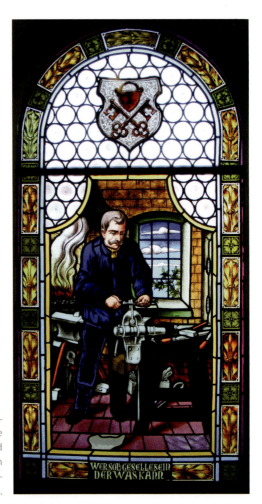

The windows of the Chamber of Crafts and Trades in Schwerin show various occupational qualifications.

Internet tip:
www.hwk-schwerin.de

found. The well-known glass pictures decorating the residence of the Chamber of Handicrafts in Friedensstrasse in Schwerin were also created by the glass artist Königsberg.

Rügen man dug right across Sweden

Millennium construction displaced
Danish customs officers

A clever idea saved Sweden a pile of money. The Kattegat region owes its Göta Canal to the creativity and ambition of Baltzar Bogislaus von Platen. The scion of a noble Rügen family had the waterway dug through the country.

Born in May 1766 on an estate near Schaprode, the thirteen-year-old Baltzar found his way to Southern Sweden, to the Karlskrona Cadet School. In 1788, he fought for Sweden at the Battle of Hogland and was temporarily taken prisoner by the Russians.

In 1801, the Admiral took over the command of the Trollhätte Canal. The waterway has joined Sweden's west coast to Lake Vänern inland since 1779. During his archive studies, Platen found drafts and sketches of a canal which would even reach as far as the east coast. He immediately recognised the economic and strategic significance of this and "took a map of Sweden, / drew a cord so blue / from east unto the west…" Thus versified an unknown author around 1880.

With a bold stroke the Göta Canal was once said to have been planned by Balthzar von Platen.

The later Göta Canal did not merely shorten the route between the western and eastern parts of the country; it also saved the Swedish ships from paying the Danish toll incurred in south Öresund. Von Platen explored the route on his own initiative and at his own expense and submitted a paper to Gustaf VI Adolf in 1806. The

For nearly 70 years the canal was an important artery for traffic.

king gave the starting signal for the project two years later and gave command of it to its initiator. Von Platen soon advanced to the Privy Council and Imperial Governor. He pushed through his construction with ambition, an iron will and sometimes in a questionable manner. He is supposed to have driven on the 60,000 workers with a cudgel, as it says in the poem. Platen himself only experienced the completion of the western section of the canal. The section between Lake Vättern and the east coast was only completed in 1832, 3 years after his death. The Swedes carried their canal builder to his grave in Motala, a town on the bank of his waterway.

For 68 years ships passed through the 58 locks, thereby almost effortlessly overcoming 91.8 metres ground level elevation. The Swedish millennial construction is a tourist attraction today.

Family members of the famous master builder still live on the Baltic Sea island of Rügen today. Anyone who would like to hear his lively success story from them has the option of lodging directly with the von Platen family in one of the holiday flats at Gut Reischvitz.

Internet tip:
www.gotakanal.se

Rostockers build library in Kenya

Association enables children
to go to school

Little Zawadi sits on a wooden bench, glued to the board. Forty little arms shoot into the air like lightning when the teacher asks for an answer. Zawadi, like each of her 39 primary school classmates, wants it to be her turn. Thanks to the "Friends of the Sabaki School", the girl from the Kikuyu tribe in Kenya can go to third grade instead of working in the fields. Eight euros a month sponsorship finances her attendance at the school and relieves her mother and seriously ill father of the school fees.

In Kenya, a country where over half the population lives on less than one dollar a day, daily school attendance is not a matter of course. In Zawadi's case, school attendance had previously been inconceivable. Her father is sick with tuberculosis and her mother has to bear the costs of her and her sisters on her own.

Deeply affected by these difficult living conditions, a group of Rostockers, who were travelling along the Sabaki river in the coastal region of Kenya, decided to found the society "Freunde der Sabaki Schule, Kenia e.V." in 1999. The most important goal of the society is to enable the children to have a school education, in order perhaps to offer them the chance of better living conditions.

A lot has happened since then. The rain no longer comes in through the school roof and the wooden floor prevents the abecedarians

Eight euros a month make it possible for Zawadi to attend school.

Internet tip: www.sabaki-schule.de

from getting their feet cold. Books and pens have been bought, with the help of which Zawadi and her fellow pupils have learned to write and calculate. It has even proved possible to build a library, which is permanently crammed.

A further project is running in Samburu District, in Kenya's hot hinterland. Juliane Thieme from Rostock is on the spot here several times a year. It is the homeland of the colourfully apparelled, semi-nomadic Samburu people. Here too, tots now write and calculate assiduously.

The Rostock society members are keen to pass on their enthusiasm. Young people can take part in work camp assignments in Kenya. With their help, school and schoolchildren can be equipped with the essentials and Rostock student teachers can practise their craft in lessons. The next target is a permanent building for school dinners. The society also organises sponsorships, as in Zawadi's case.

In the on-site projects, the Rostockers are sometimes confronted by difficult tasks. The tropical heat, the simple conditions of life and communication problems demand a lot of them. In the end, though, pleasure in the hospitality, the fascination of the tradition-steeped cultures and the magnificent scenery always win out. The work of the young people from Rostock is successful: each child that manages to break out of the vicious circle of a lack of education and poverty makes their efforts worthwhile.

Euro visionary in 1909

Mecklenburg chemist launched first
international currency

His name is virtually forgotten, his exact place of birth a mystery, but his vision lives: as early as 1909 in London, the emigrant from Mecklenburg, industrial chemist and Esperanto activist Herbert F. Höveler (1859-1918), implemented the trendsetting idea of a neutral currency. Without decades of political fuss and without all-embracing Brussels red tape. Under the name "Chekbanko Esperantista" Höveler founded a financial institute which allowed its customers to make cheap and uncomplicated financial transfers between more than 40 countries all over the world, reports Esperanto chronicler Ralf Kuse from Schwerin. The currency, obviously called Speso – derived from the French espèce: "coin" – was coupled to the gold price. "A Spesmilo had a gold value of 0.8 grams and was redeemable in English pounds with a cheque inscribed with Esperanto texts in every bank in the world", is how the author of many publications about Höveler explains the principle.

The value of the smaller Spescento was set in similarly creative and practicable fashion. It was the equivalent value of a stamp for a letter abroad.

Anyhow, in 1914, 730 customers in 320 towns in 43 countries were resorting to Höveler's farsighted global currency.

The Euro precursor, today almost forgotten in his homeland, is still highly regarded in specialist circles. "Höveler ventured a utopia then that has only become reality today", points out the Vienna expert Herbert Mayer. According to the Director of the Constructed Language Collection and the Esperanto Museum in the Austrian National Library, this makes him "one of the more significant personalities in the history of Esperanto". What is really well-known, however, is not the creator, but the Speso itself. Both are also immortalised in the world's largest constructed language collection. Between 30,000 volumes of books and thousands of posters and exhibits such as Esperanto stars or flags, there lies in a display cabinet in the "Utopias" section an inconspicuous piece of paper commemorating present remittance slips. With his purposeful implementation of the idea hatched shortly before by the Swiss mathematician René de Saussure of an international currency on the basis of the decimal system, the Mecklenburger in London was far ahead of his time.

And not just that: the founder of the London Esperanto Club, still active today, and other language clubs in Italy and Palestine, also published along the way a successful summary of Esperanto grammar. And he even made his beloved regional writer Fritz Reuter accessible to the Esperanto world. The result is called Kio povas okazi, se oni donacas surprize – in good Low German Wat bi 'ne Äwerraschung 'ruter kamen kann. Höveler even engaged his own illustrator for his Reuter translation, which is also incidentally in Vienna.

The visionary currency may have died at that time with the death of Höveler in the First World War, as there was nobody to continue it. But Höveler's Speso lives on. The depiction of

Internet tips:
www.esperanto-gb.org
www.esperanto-usa.org

At one time a Speso note could be exchanged for English pounds.

the notes continues to turn up as before at every international Esperanto congress, says Dr Martin Haase, Director of the German Esperanto Institute (DEI). Questions about Spesmilo & Co. are still among the standard repertoire of the higher Esperanto language exams today. And until very recently the formula for calculating the current Speso value was still to be found in every Esperantist yearbook. "Even though the person of Höveler may have been somewhat eclipsed", says the DEI head, "the Speso is simply part of Esperanto culture."

This had obviously not penetrated all the political palaver about the introduction of the Euro as afar as a few outstanding Deutschmark hard-liners, principally from the Bajuvarian Free State. "Some there fulminated about the allegedly worthless Esperanto money", chuckles the Vienna expert Mayer. "They probably still don't know today that it really existed."

Astronomer with a golden nose

Tycho Brahe got his trademark in Rostock

Rostock University produced a scientist who had a good nose in the field of astronomy, but in the literal sense it was a false one. For the Dane Tycho Brahe was one of the world's first wearers of an artificial nose.

The Rostock student lost his own nose in a dispute about his mathematical abilities. In 1566, he argued with a fellow student about who of them was the better mathematician. To settle the matter they decided to hold a duel, in which Brahe's nose fell victim to a sharp blow of his opponent's rapier. He was immediately fitted with an artificial nose made of an alloy of gold and silver. This prosthesis became his trademark.

After this unfortunate event Brahe remained in Rostock for two more years, until 1568. He lived for a while at the home of Levinus Battus, Professor of Medicine at the University. It is reputed that Battus awakened his interest in medicine and alchemy.

Brahe had begun his academic career at the early age of 13, studying not only law but also the humanities and natural sciences at Leipzig, Wittenberg, Rostock and Basle. A total eclipse of the sun in the early 1560s had so fascinated him that he decided to devote his whole life to the study of the stars. He continued his meticulous records of his astronomical observations for nearly four decades.

In 1570 he returned to his native Denmark. Two years later, he described changes in the constellation of Cassiopeia. He had discovered a supernova, a new star. This observation caused a major stir, for at that time it was generally thought that the firmament was static and unchanging. Brahe disproved this idea in his book "De Nova Stella" (1573), which made him famous across Europe.

Brahe was also revolutionary in realising that the instruments available in his day for observing the stars did not provide accurate results. He therefore developed new methods for the precise measurement of the positions of the heavenly bodies. He made the instruments of metal and as large as possible, so as to achieve more precise results through the use of a larger scale. However, Brahe was not yet able to use a telescope. Galileo Galilei did not discover the benefits of using curved lenses until eight years after Brahe's death.

A relief on the gable of a house in Rostock recalls Tycho Brahe.

His scientific achievements did not, however, prevent him being at odds with the Danish royal court, which resulted in Brahe leaving his homeland in 1597. He entered into the service of Emperor Rudolf II in Prague. His assistant there was none other than Johannes Kepler, who continued Brahe's investigations after the latter's death in 1601.

On the Danish island of Ven, where Brahe had previously worked, the remains of Brahe's Uraniborg observatory can still be seen, and one can visit the restored Stjerneborg observatory or the museum in the former All Saints Church. The Hanseatic City of Rostock also honours its famous student: a street and the astronomical centre are named after him. There is also a relief depicting the astronomer on the gable of a house in Garbräterstrasse. His golden nose is clearly to be seen there, too.

Internet tips:
www.tychobrahe.com
www.tycho.dk

Fallen hero of the skies

Otto Lilienthal from Anklam laid the groundwork for modern aviation

A huge wooden bat glides through the air. The multitude throngs on the ground while holding their breath for the romantic visionary daring his neck: aviation pioneer Otto Lilienthal (1848-1896) is testing one of his flying contraptions.

From 1891 to 1896, Lilienthal was the first person to try out gliding flight successfully and repeatedly with a total of 21 homemade aircraft. Starting out from a specially heaped-up hill, he manoeuvred the prototypes through the air, steered by shifting his own body weight. A method still used by the pilots of modern hang gliders today.

The man from Anklam was a graduate mechanical engineer and inventor. He puzzled out numerous machines, including many steam boilers and engines, and filed 25 patents, four of them on his flying objects. He built multifarious gadgetry to measure pressure and air conditions.

The instructors of the visionary were the birds themselves. He studied the flight of storks and transferred his observations to the drawing-board. Lilienthal experimented for all of 23 years before trying out his first aircraft, built by himself. With constant improvements to his equipment, he laid the groundwork for present-day aviation.

The aviation pioneer published his findings in numerous publications and articles. He received domestic and foreign aviation pioneers to technical discussions in Berlin, among their number Samuel Pierpont Langley from the USA, Nikolai Egorovich Schukovsky from Russia, Percy Pilcher from England and Wilhelm Kress from Austria. Sensational photographs of Lilienthal's trials appeared in the scientific and popular publications around the globe.

In 1881, Lilienthal set up an aircraft factory. The entrepreneur was not just innovative at the technical level, he was also committed in the artistic and social spheres. He let his at times 60 employees share in the profits, for instance. And he saw the dream of the airplane as a means of international understanding and of eternal peace.

Lilienthal's vision came to a sudden end on 9th August 1896 near Stölln at the Gollenberg. He suffered fatal injuries in a crash. Many aviation pioneers, however, continued to work according to his methods and principles. In December 1903, the Wright brothers tested the first successful engine-powered airplane.

Lilienthal-Museum
Ellbogenstraße 1
17389 Anklam
Tel. +49(0)3971 245500
www.lilienthal-museum.de

This photograph was taken in 1894 during Otto Lilienthal's trials on his flight hill.

Concrete with pizazz

Ulrich Müther created a furore with daring roof constructions

Water Lily, Scallop or Maple Leaf – charming names for buildings of concrete. The Binz architect Ulrich Müther adopted the forms of North German nature and developed special techniques to subjugate the cement mixture. The construction method that Müther helped to develop attracted attention abroad as well and brought the former GDR valuable currency. The constructions were treasured in the socialist republic. They brought bold variety to the square-cut prefabricated high-rise landscape and were economical as well.

Müther completed his degree on the calculation of curved surfaces, hyperbolic paraboloids, in Dresden in 1963, thus laying the foundations for his elegant hypar-shell constructions. A curving network of steel girders serves as a framework for the concrete, which is sprayed on in layers. Müther built an unusual escape tower in Binz, for example, properties in Potsdam and Berlin, and created a landmark in Rostock-Warnemünde: the "Teepott" (teapot) – references which led to commissions abroad. Working together with the prize GDR exporter Carl Zeiss Jena, Müther die cast for planetaria in Helsinki, Kuwait, Algiers and Tripoli. Carl Zeiss Jena supplied the technology, Müther the appropriate concrete domes. He also constructed the bob sled course in Oberhof. It was the first in the world to be constructed without any frame. Cycling tracks in Havana, Szczecin and Rostock also bear Müther's signature.

As the GDR disappeared, however, so too did interest in Müther's architecture and his concrete buildings. Some buildings were razed, others are becoming derelict. All the protests against demolition were no help to the Maple Leaf in Berlin; on the other hand, the Warnemünde Teepott was saved. It has stood next to the lighthouse since 1968 as a landmark, and if you will, as a memorial to the concrete shell constructor Ulrich Müther as well, who died in August 2007 at the age of 72.

The "Teepott" is a landmark of Warnemünde.

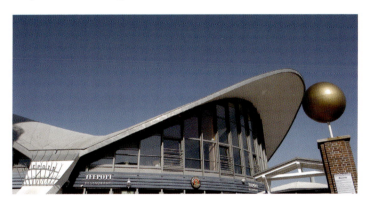

Intercultural masterpiece in Güstrow

European builders shaped
castle architecture

Cultural imports in Mecklenburg-Western Pomerania are by no means merely a question of French or Italian designer labels. A magnificent building in the federal state reflects the influences from Italy, France and even the Netherlands by its architecture.

At first glance, Güstrow Castle appears rather dreamy. It is enthroned before the castle pond, along whose banks the willow branches project in melancholy fashion into the water. On looking closer, the alert spirit detects a lively past. The Renaissance building from the 16th century is the architectural icing on the cake of the otherwise rather classicist-style town.

From 1558, the master builder from Lombardy, Franziskus Parr, and later the Dutchman Brandin fashioned a half-burnt-down castle into a four-wing ensemble. Parr was commissioned by Duke Ulrich of Mecklenburg after he had taken office in 1557. The architecture of the south and west wings is reminiscent of that of his Lombardy homeland. The Duke returned from a trip to Italy deeply impressed by Mediterranean architecture. The dominance of Italian artistic and architectural elements in his building were supposed emphatically to underscore the power of the Duke.

From 1587 to 1588, Brandin created the north wing in the clearer and more severe Dutch manner. His assistant Claus Midow completed the

Internet tips:
www.schloss-guestrow.de
www.mecklenburgische-schweiz.de

encirclement of the inner courtyard with the construction of the east wing in 1594. Work was only completed in 1671 with the erection of the gate lodge in front of the west wing by the Frenchman Charles Philippe Dieussart. The turrets, corner designs and plastic wall arrangements still give the castle a French touch today, recalling the banks of the Loire.

Anyone wishing to be enchanted by the cultural conflations can go on a voyage of discovery through the castle. From 1628 to 1629, no less a person than Albrecht von Wallenstein resided in the building.

Today, the former rulers' seat Güstrow Castle is a favoured tourist attraction.

Martha – music from Mecklenburg

Teutendorf virtuoso composed in Paris and Vienna

The Mecklenburg composer Friedrich von Flotow composed music that has been heard around the world, even if his name is well known only to the musical cognoscenti. One of his most famous pieces, "The last rose of summer" from the opera "Martha", is, today, virtually a folksong and belongs to the repertoire of popular virtuosos such as André Rieu. Friedrich von Flotow came into the world in April 1812, in the paternal manor in Teutendorf in Mecklenburg. To comply with the wishes of his strict father, Flotow initially aspired to be a diplomat, but soon gave it up in favour of his music. In 1828, he even left his Mecklenburg homeland, with his father's consent, to have lessons in the musical metropolis of Paris with the composer Anton Reicha.

Paris inspired Flotow to write numerous compositions. Many of his sound creations were performed for private circles of enthusiasts. In the thirties, together with the still largely unknown Jacques Offenbach, Flotow captivated the soiree sets of aristocratic and moneyed Paris. There he also maintained contact with the leading musicians of the city, including Charles Gounod and Gioacchino Rossini. He assisted Pasticcion in his compositions and became increasingly popular. His first opera "Pierre et Cathérine" was performed at the ducal theatre (Schwerin Hoftheater) and the Mecklenburg

Friedrich von Flotow celebrated international successes in the 19th century.

court in Ludwigslust in 1835. In 1938, all Paris celebrated Flotow's "Le Naufrage de la Méduse" after its performance at the Théatre de la Renaissance. This huge success paved the composer's way to the Grand Opéra. Fame was heaped upon him in Germany, too, after "Alessandro Stradella" premièred at the Hamburg Stadttheater in 1844 and was later staged at 15 other theatres within the same year.

Flotow's fame brought him a commission from the Vienna Hoftheater. The opera "Martha, or The Fair at Richmond" proceeded triumphantly through the whole of Europe, following its first performance on 25th November 1847.

Despite his international successes, Friedrich von Flotow returned to Mecklenburg-Western Pomerania, the revolution having driven the composer out of his adopted country France. He settled at Wutzig estate and wedded Elise von Zadow. Here, he was so inspired by his home environment that he composed such works as "Die Grossfürstin Sophia Katharina". After a stay in Vienna, Flotow returned to Schwerin in 1855 as director of court music and the court theatre. Here, he built up the orchestra.

After the collapse of his second marriage, Flotow married the singer Rosa Theen, and the restless globetrotter withdrew to an estate near Vienna in 1868. He undertook trips to Paris, London and Berlin and continued composing: "Am Runenstein", "L'Ombre" and "La Fleur d'Harlem" were performed by opera houses in Prague, Paris and Turin.

The musician composed his later works at his father's estate in Teutendorf. He spent his final years at the Heiligenkreuzberg estate near Darmstadt, where he died in January 1883.

Internet tip:
www.festspiele-mv.de

Stallion in Napoleon's service

White horse from Ivenack as loot in France

The stallion Herodot persists in a thousand year old oak tree. Hidden here, he is supposed to avoid capture by Napoleon's forces. But then … The coveted stallion was the head of an entire herd of mares of the stud horse Ivenack in Mecklenburg, whose impeccable reputation had resounded in far away Paris. After Napoleon marched into Mecklenburg, he allowed the splendid specimen to be confiscated, in order to, if anything, enhance the value of his own horse breeding, that was said to be only moderately effective.

Herodot had been taken to safety in a timely manner. Admittedly, the white horse felt so drawn to his herd of mares that he neighed and betrayed his concealment when the mares were lead past the oak tree. Thus, the valuable stallion was lost to his herd – temporarily.

According to a legend, this horse was hidden in a tree.

It was rumoured that Herodot was to have had a formidable career. He was supposed to have carried the Empress Josephine on his back. It is said, that he fought battles with Napoleon, who developed an apparent fascination with the white horse.

Herodot experienced the end of the war on French soil and, as a matter of fact, thereby wrote a little piece of world history. In 1815, on the verge of the Vienna Congress, Field Marshall von Blücher sought to secure permission to return Herodot to Mecklenburg. According to historical sources, by authorisation of the Field Marshall, Herodot was confiscated at the Harbour of Marseilles and ridden all the way back home.

Even today, a bust on the gable of the stables in Ivenack memorialises the most famous offspring of the two breeding horses Morwick Ball and Herodias who made it all the way into France. The entire, so-called French period, when Napoleon's troops occupied Mecklenburg, is on display at the castle's vaults in Stavenhagen. There is also a picture of Herodot here to be marvelled at. In spite of his eventful life, or because of it, the horse reached 35 years of age and is supposed to have been buried under a thousand year old oak tree.

> Fritz-Reuter-Literaturmuseum
> Markt 1
> 17153 Stavenhagen
> Tel. +49(0)39954 21072
> www.fritz-reuter-literaturmuseum.de

Green tea in a red pavilion

A touch of chinoiserie – not far
from the Baltic Sea

Everything happens fifty years later in Mecklenburg-Western Pomerania, Chancellor Otto von Bismarck is once said to have stated. And indeed the chinoiserie of the 18th century arrived late at the Baltic Sea. Duke Friedrich Franz I of Mecklenburg-Schwerin had two pavilions built after the Chinese model at the Kamp, at the heart of Bad Doberan, at the beginning of the 19th century.

No less a person than the important architect Carl Theodor Severin designed the two octagonal teahouses. The Red Pavilion was built in 1809, its white counterpart, two-storeyed and stylishly surrounded by pillars, followed in 1813. Friedrich Franz I and his entourage used it as a music salon. Since 1976, the pretty classicist construction with the Chinese touch has been taking guests as a restaurant and café. In the tower room you can still feast as regally today as in the times of Friedrich Franz. Chinese green tea is also served by request. The Red Pavilion, with its curved roof, is today home to the gallery of the art society of the same name. Artists from the region regularly exhibit in the historic octagon.

Art after the Chinese model reached the duchy of Mecklenburg-Strelitz even later. However, Mecklenburg-Strelitz had no wish to be inferior in any way to the neighbouring dukedom. Grand Duke Georg commissioned the Schinkel follower Friedrich Wilhelm Buttel to erect

Kunstverein Roter
Pavillon e.V.
Am Kamp
18209 Bad Doberan
Tel. +49(0)38203
12404

a Chinese pavilion in 1821. The wooden jewel, which his Highness probably never saw from inside, as it functioned as a rinse house for the ducal washing, stands right on the edge of Lake Zierk. Today the pavilion is a listed building and, apart from the two pavilions in Bad Doberan, the only surviving building in the Mecklenburg-Western Pomerania in the chinoiserie style.

Anyone interested in architecture with an Asian touch should definitely pay a visit to the koi temple in Lelkendorf, erected by koi enthusiast Martin Scholz. The society of the colourful fish can also be enjoyed for rather longer: there is a cosy holiday flat in the attic.

Internet tips:
www.bad-doberan.de
www.neustrelitz.de

The Kamp in Bad Doberan around 1855

New home of the dragon boat

Schwerin firm delivers all over the World

Mecklenburg-Western Pomerania won the international dragon boat world cup in Sydney. Regardless which team from which nation dashed to first place along the home stretch, a dragon boat from the Baltic Sea coast was be out in front. The dragon boats from all the various countries which lined up on the start line in the world cup in September 2007 were initially launched in Lübesse near Schwerin. The company "Boots- und Kunststoffbau GmbH (BuK)" is the only producer of dragon boats in Germany, and worldwide market leader. BuK's dragon boat design is now considered the international racing standard dragon boat worldwide. Certified by the International al Dragon Boat association, the firm sends top-quality branded goods to North America, Australia and even to the home of dragon boat sports: to Asia.

The first boats were brought onto the market by the BuK at the beginning of the 90s. The slender 22-seater is still to this day constructed based on the historical boat measurements. Not only has the company built a bridge between past and the present, but also between Asia and the rest of the world.

Dragon boat racing's popularity is no longer confined to just the Asian continent. The sport dates back to the first famous Chinese poet Chu Yuan. He is supposed to have drowned in the year 300 B.C. in the Mi Lo river, despite

Internet tips:
www.buk-gmbh.de
www.drachenboot-festival.de

the efforts of the villagers to save him from the giant fish by their drumbeats. Every year since the poet has been celebrated with the dragon boat races.

Since the 90's, Mecklenburg-Western Pomerania's capital Schwerin has established itself as a genuine stronghold for dragon boats. With the Dragon Boat Festival, the resident city organises year after year the biggest festival of its kind in all of Europe. Every year more than 100 dragon boats battle for victory on Lake Pfaffenteich. For 3 days it is swarming with visitors, who cheer on their favourites and who cannot pass up all the various highlights the festival has to offer. For a more personal dragon boat experience, BuK has created an extra large boat, which can be rented upon request. This construction is unique in all Europe and almost double the size of the normal dragon boat. It offers space for up to 54 paddlers.

The dragon boat races popular today go back to an old tradition which originated on the Mi-Lo river.

Underwater treasure hunt

Did a Barth shipowner construct the first diving suit?

Internet tips:
www.stadt-barth.de
www.kulturportal-mv.de
www.mecklenburg-vorpommern.de

Peter Kreeft from Pomerania is alleged to have developed an enclosed diving suit some 30 years before the Deane brothers, who are today considered the inventors (1828).

As early as 1800 Kreeft had already tried out the suit in the Bodden. 5 years later an onlooker had set down his observations in writing. He apparently attended Peter Kreefts dive, who dared the high tides in order to salvage copper plates from a wreckage. The suit was highly innovative. In order to prevent the infiltration of water, the suit was enclosed. The helmet consisted of iron rods, coated with waterproof leather. Kreeft also added useful extras: a voice communications system which maintained contact with the surface and a flexible tube, which transported used air out and fresh air in, brought a level of comfort to diving which had been unknown up until this point. Kreeft further developed his diving suit and a couple of years later exhibited it in Stralsund. In the meantime he had incorporated led plates in the the soles of the boots, in order to combat ascending forces – a method which was utilised well into the 20th century. Kreeft himself may have found a profitable use from his invention. Unfortunately he did not apply for a patent and was therefore denied glory and fame.

A contemporary drawing captures Peter Kreeft's innovative suit for posterity.

Tragic End off Tokyo

Prussian schooner sank on diplomatic mission

On 18th October 1990, the town of Wolgast celebrated three ships of the Frauenlob class, putting in to the harbour for the first time in almost 135 years. The keel of the first "Frauenlob" (praise of women) was laid down in the shipyard in 1851. To procure the necessary financial means for building an effective navy, the women of Prussia in the mid 19th century collected for a war schooner. The collection boxes of the women of Wolgast were particularly well filled. Not least for this reason, the well-known shipyard received the commission from the Admiralty to build the war schooner. It was to bear the name "Frauengabe" (gift of women) in honour of the diligent collectors.

Museen der Stadt Wolgast
Rathausplatz 6
17438 Wolgast
Tel. +49(0)3836 203041

After local celebrities such as the pioneer of German iron shipbuilding, Rudolf Haak, had assisted shipbuilder Lübke in the construction of the schooner, Admiral Prince Adalberg of Prussia gave himself the personal honour of launching the vessel. At the request of his father, King Friedrich Wilhelm IV, he announced a change of name for the schooner to "Frauenlob", which was also sealed in traditional fashion with a bottle of wine on the bow. On the 1st May 1856, the schooner entered service and already in her first year it was setting sail to safeguard Prussian trade relations.

Shipbuilding went through a real boom in the mid 19th century. The great powers were striv-

A model of the "Frauenlob" can be seen in the Wolgast museum "Kaffeemühle".

Internet tips:
www.wolgast.de
www.museum.wolgast.de

ing for commercial settlements in China. They sought for the opening up of Japanese ports for international maritime traffic. When the ports of Nagasaki, Kanagawa and Hokadate were due to be opened, Prussia sent a squadron at the turn of the year 1859/1860 to Japan, of which the "Frauenlob" was one. In the following late summer, the sailing frigate "Thetis", the steam frigate "Arcona", and the Wolgast schooner reached the Japanese coast.

But the little squadron strays into a typhoon before Yokohama. On 1st September, the situation for the "Frauenlob" becomes threatening. With the utmost effort, the exhausted crews set up a tow connection with the "Arcona". But raging waters bring the situation out of control. The towline breaks. The "Frauenlob" is on its own. On the morning of the 2nd September, the schooner is out of sight before the bay of Yeddo (today Tokyo). Lost together with the ship were four officers, a doctor and forty-one men. Today, the missing crew is commemorated by memorial plaques in the Marine-Garnison churches of Kiel and Wilhelmshaven.

The "Arcona" completed the Prussian squadron's mission. On 4th September, the Prussian envoys hoisted the Prussian flag in Yeddo. Six naval ships followed the "Frauenlob" onto the slipway of the Wolgast Lübke shipyard – and all were spared a fate such as that befell the "Frauenlob".

Diva at the "Karusel"

Asta Nielsen relaxed at the
Isle of Hiddensee

White on blue, with just one S and one L – that's how the name "Karusel" appears in Asta Nielsen's native language on the house wall above the door. The Danish silent film star relaxed in bohemian society at the semicircular building in the "oasis in the Baltic Sea" (Nielsen) in the 1920s.

The diva was drawn to her enchanting Hiddensee hideout in the summers between 1925 and 1933. "Under inconceivably high and blue heavens, immersed in light and colours", Asta Nielsen received sculptors, poets and actor colleagues at her "Karusel"; Gerhart Hauptmann, Paul Wegener, Joachim Ringelnatz and many more. She served cracknel from the island baker, smoked eel, flounder and punch. By request of the actress, each visitor in return left a plant in the garden of the house.

A request the Ringelnatz family took a little too literally: When the hostess returned to her "Karusel" after a lengthy bathe in the Baltic Sea, she found the grass garden completely disfigured. Her friends had managed to construct a kind of park with paths and cairns out of the pretty piece of nature. Now they were just putting caraway, onions, dates, lemons and Brazil nuts in the remaining patches of earth. When the first shock was over, the Dane took the whole thing with humour, for she felt nowhere "as young, as happy and as free as on this island".

Joachim Ringelnatz counted among the guests of Asta Nielsen on Hiddensee.

Internet tip:
www.brightlights-film.com

This jewel from the drawing table of the architect Max Taut, whose charm enchants lovers of Hiddensee as it once did the silent film star Asta Nielsen, is still found by visitors today, hidden in a high coppice, on the outskirts of the little village of Vitte.

State-of-the-art at 60

Rostock and Wismar send ships to the seven seas

Container giants with the names "Stadt Wismar" and "Stadt Rostock" shuttle between the USA, the Mediterranean and India. Cutting-edge constructions built in Mecklenburg-Western Pomerania, the bow in Rostock/Warnemünde, the stern in Wismar.
Mecklenburg-Western Pomerania's shipyards are among the most modern in the world. The concerns in Rostock and Wismar have been producing one ocean giant after another for what is now 60 years.
They are an important driving force on the European market. The joint company Aker Yards links Rostock and Wismar to shipyards in Brazil, Romania, Norway, Ukraine, Finland and France.

The Peene Shipyard in Wolgast produces naval vessels, but is also active in civilian shipbuilding today.

The 900th ship was launched from the Wismar Aker shipyard in July 2006. The shipbuilding plants have delivered 74 different types of ship all over the world and still the order books are full.

Aker Yards are part of the Aker group, a multinational concern based in Oslo with more than 50,000 employees. The concern has bundled the capacities of the Mecklenburg sites and made the shipyards of Wismar and Rostock Warnemünde into a genuine international centre of excellence.

The product range stretches from cruisers and ferries through offshore and special ships to container ships. A third of all new commissions in Germany are for container ships, which are only built in Rostock and Wismar, and the Volkswerft shipyard in Stralsund. This has made Mecklenburg-Western Pomerania an essential hub for the future industry of shipbuilding and commercial shipping in Germany, Europe and on the international market.

The Stralsund Volkswerft offers ideal conditions and the latest systems, continuing the centuries-old tradition of shipbuilding in Stralsund and producing mainly for the Maersk shipping company in Sweden. Besides, the shipyard Peene-Werft GmbH in Wolgast has established an excellent reputation within 50 years of existence. It has delivered more than 700 new constructed ships all over the world.

Internet tips:
www.akeryards.com
www.volkswerft.de
www.peene-werft.hegemann-gruppe.de

Mecklenburg Statue of Liberty

Mirow princess at the American east coast

Just like the Statue of Liberty, a Mecklenburg princess lifts her arm into the sky – right in front of the terminal building at Charlotte international airport in the state of North Carolina. The North American town is named for Charlotte Sophia, born to the duchy of Mecklenburg-Strelitz, who became Queen of the United Kingdom in 1761. In 1990, Raymon Kaskey created a statue in her honour that still greets visitors at the airport to this day.

In 1768, the settlers who named their newly built town Charlotte were either enchanted by Her Majesty or were, perhaps, hoping to gain favour of the king. Even her Mecklenburg homeland's name was taken to the New World. Since 1757, the area surrounding modern Charlotte has been referred to as Mecklenburg County. In order to establish a partnership not only in name, the German original Mecklenburg-Western Pomerania and its North American counterpart concluded an agreement on 19th January 1994 in order to initiate specific projects. Within the partnership agreement, the small Mecklenburg town of Mirow, the birthplace of Queen Charlotte, established a place of information where visitors are invited to learn about Her Majesty and the special partnership of both the Mecklenburgs. More precise details may be found at the so called Torhaus of the castle complex.

A statue of Sophie Charlotte greets air passengers in North Carolina.

Internet tip:
www.northcarolina-consularcorps.org
www.charmeck.org

Hanseatic soccer school in Chicago

Ex-Hansa player trains youngsters in the USA

"Hansa Soccer Academy" – an unusual name for a Chicago football school. It was so named by the ex-professional Thomas Gansauge. The footballer still feels the ties with his home club FC Hansa Rostock, that he played for between 1996 and 1999, and so took the name abroad with him. He trains young talents at the academy, which he founded with his partner, Jakub Lisek, in 2006. Lisek comes from Chicago and was Gansauge's teammate – not at FC Hansa, but at FC Rot-Weiss Erfurt. Then, the idea of opening a soccer school was first adumbrated. The footballers realised their dream in Chicago later. And the Hansa Soccer Academy is a complete success: more than 150 children register for the summer camps.

Incidentally, to keep in shape, the ex-professional still plays occasionally for "Schwaben A.C." This club was founded by immigrants to the United States as well, however already in 1926.

Internet tip:
www.hansasoccer.com

Thomas Gansauge trains young soccer talents in the USA.

Of bockwurst and beer in Brazil

South America's Pomeranian tradition

According to his name, Albert Ramlow could be from Greifswald. Indeed, the man from Brazil is tracing his roots in the Hanseatic town.

His great-great-grandparents were driven by poverty out of Pomerania to South America almost 150 years ago, to Pomerode. Many thousands left their Pomeranian homeland in order to escape its nuisances. The name already points unmistakably to the founders, of which Albert's grandfather was one. The Pomeranians cleared (German: roden) the country to make it habitable. Some of Pomeroder's 23,000 inhabitants still live in houses whose architecture recalls the North German. No monumental buildings but pretty half-timbered houses line the streets. Some German-Brazilians lovingly named them "homesick houses" that were made from brick in a traditional manner. Visitors to the town are appealed to farmhouses even before entering the mediaeval town gate. Many of them were built by Egon Tiedt, the operator of the Pomeranian Museum.

Houses in Pomerode tell the story of German immigrants.

Pomerode was founded on 21st January 1861. Roughly 350,000 Pomeranians emigrated between 1840 and 1918. The Brazilian government offered seed capital, land and property, exemption from military service and religious freedom – an incredible offer for many destitute people from the Prussian province. They left their homeland but they did not leave their culture behind. Each year, in the birth month of the town in Itajai Valley, 30,000 people celebrate a noisy Pomerania festival. They cultivate old customs for ten days, with street processions, folklore and folk music. And once the champions of traditional games have been awarded, there is a solid Pomeranian meal: duck and red cabbage, bockwurst, knuckle of pork and freshly tapped cool beer.

Albert had accompanied his uncle enthusiastically at his forays through the history of Pomerode. This makes him all the happier that in recent years a partnership has come into being between Pomerode and Greifswald. The towns' mayors want to deepen the contact in order to create multifaceted economic links. Brazilian representatives, for example, attended the opening of the regional museum "Pommersches Landesmuseum" in Greifswald in October 2001. As a sign of friendship, Albert bequeathed the museum a special treasure: the actual papers of his great-great-grandfather. Two years later, Greifswald's mayor followed an invitation to Brazil.

Albert enjoys visiting his ancestor's homeland. He likes the snow and the bald trees in wintertime, the smell of rape in spring and the short summer nights. He has no linguistic problems here. The globetrotter can even converse with the older people of Western Pomerania in Low German.

The Brazilian has big plans in Pomerode, wants to write a book and perhaps issue a DVD about what he has discovered in modern Western Pomerania. By the way, the German-Brazilian's real name is Alberto – but it is not one he likes to hear.

Internet tip:
www.pomerodeon-line.com

Pommersches Landesmuseum
Rakower Str. 9
17489 Greifswald
Tel. +49(0)3834 83120

Ribnitz – scenery for comic series

Feininger captured Mecklenburg and Pomerania

1906. Sunday after Sunday, the Chicago Tribune writes about a small town in Mecklenburg-Western Pomerania. Comic hero Willie Winkie scurries around between little houses that wink at him with their window eyes and smile at him with their door mouths. The clock tower of the town church of St. Marien, in the role of a custodian, keeps a watchful eye on the colourful cluster of little houses. No less a person than Lyonel Feininger drew these comics in, which he based on the townscape of Ribnitz and into which he wove in masterly fashion the characteristics of the town on the Baltic Sea. A year later, the Chicago Sunday Tribune presented them in the comic series "Wee Willie Winkie's World".

The painter had spent some of the loveliest weeks of his life by the Baltic Sea together with his future wife Julia. Fascinated by the magical idyll of the small town, he immortalised Ribnitz and the coastal region in over 20 works. Here he found his typical style, with architecture as the dominant picture motif and crystalline forms. Julia Feininger lamented as much as the artist himself that the inspirational place was so far away: "Oh, and our dear Ribnitz ... It was a magical town and it's magically far away." (Julia Feininger in a letter to Lyonel, October 1905)
Feininger spent entire summers in the Baltic Sea region, enthused by the architecture of its

old towns. He made his first pilgrimage to Rügen as early as 1892. Decades later, he was still yearning for the sea: "Pommern and the Baltic Sea were ever present in my entire creativity and I still draw on my experiences that I had there. There is nothing here that compares."

Born in New York, Lyonel Feininger was later drawn to Paris, and then to Berlin. He worked as an illustrator and cartoonist in Berlin and was summoned to Weimar in 1919 by Walter Gropius for the founding of the Bauhaus school. He subsequently moved to Dessau. Under the influence of the National Socialists he emigrated with his wife Julia Feininger back to the USA in 1933. In his native city of New York, Feininger worked from then on as a freelance painter.

Evidence of Feininger's reverence for Ribnitz-Damgarten is provided by the etching "The Gate" from 1912, one of the most important works of the German-American painter. It reproduces the Rostock Gate in Ribnitz. An original print of "The Gate" has been hanging close by its model in Ribnitz-Damgarten since 2006. Two further prints can be admired far away in important American museums. The National Gallery of Art in Washington, the Museum of Modern Art in New York and the Ribnitz-Damgarten Fine Art Society thereby guard a key work of Feininger as a common treasure.

The society honours the famous visitor to the town with exhibitions, lectures, symposia and publications. The comic series "Wee Willie Winkie's World" can be read in the Gallery in the Monastery in Ribnitz-Damgarten, which is operated by the Fine Art Society. The gallery reappraises the works and work of Lyonel Feininger in the Baltic region and confronts

Internet tip:
www.feininger-galerie.de

Galerie im Kloster des Kunstvereins Ribnitz-Damgarten e.V.
Im Kloster 9
18311 Ribnitz-Damgarten
Tel. +49(0)3821 4701

This original print of the etching "The Gate" is in the possession of the town of Ribnitz-Damgarten.

them with works by other artistic figures, thereby showing them in a new light.

The gallery is also the leading address for anybody interested in the music of Lyonel Feininger or in literature on him. On sale at the gallery is a large selection of catalogues and reference books on the life and work of the artist, even music CDs with recordings of his compositions and his own design of notepaper.

Warnemünders were Munch's models

Norwegian captured lifeguards on canvas

Edvard Munch got the inspiration for his painting "Bathing Men" in Warnemünde.

In front of the bright blue Warnemünde sky, athletic bodies are basking in the sunshine. By this motif the vanguard painter Edvard Munch captured the place of his recovery from a deep depression on canvas. Two Warnemünde lifeguards are said to have posed for his painting "Bathing Men". Upright postures and bright colours testify to his convalescence – a condition he had only just recovered living in a freely chosen exile after years of restlessness. Munch enjoyed being inspired by the sea side

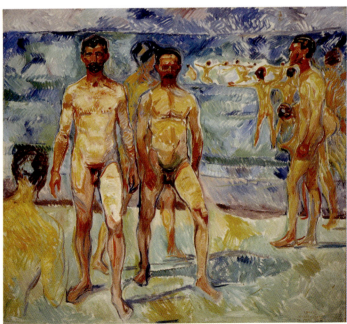

resort for several months. He had arranged his studio at the fisherman's house of the former sea pilot Carl Nielsen. His series of "The Green Room", that Munch was working on during the first few weeks he spent in Warnemünde, is full of negatively charged motifs. A few months later, however, Munch reported to the Swedish collector Ernest Thiel that he felt a new man. Enlivened by fresh air and rushing water, the pioneer of expressionism stayed by the Baltic Sea from June 1907 until October 1908.

Still today, one can trace Munch's footsteps in Warnemünde. The Edvard Munch-House Association aims at the remembrance of his work and the improvement of the understanding among nations. The Munch-House at the sea side resort has become a place to meet and communicate for German and Norwegian artists. Definitely, all of them will face the motif of bathing men as did Munch 100 years ago.

Internet tip:
www.munch.museum.no

Edvard Munch-Haus Warnemünde e.V.
Am Strom 53
18119 Warnemünde
Tel. +49(0)381 5486608

Life sciences from the coast

BioCon Valley part of a global network

The world's first artificial liver was developed by innovative researchers from Mecklenburg-Western Pomerania. It is now being used to help countless patients in more than 30 countries. This revolutionary alternative to a liver transplant is one of the successes of BioCon Valley, a working group active in the fields of life science and health economics located in Rostock, Greifswald and Groß Lüsewitz. This initiative is promoting the commercial use of modern biological and medical science and technologies.

Besides, the members of BioCon Valley also work at cross-border level. The group works hand in hand with biotech regions abroad. For example, the initiative is a member of the Scan-Balt alliance, a network uniting all the bioregions in the Baltic Sea area. In 2001 ScanBalt was launched as a joint EU project, helping its members to focus their interests more effectively at European level.

There is also a lively exchange of ideas with the Far East. Since 2004 the Baltic initiative has been collaborating with Medical Valley in Japan. The Hoa Lac Hi-Tech Park in Hanoi (Vietnam) is also taking advantage of the opportunities presented by the Baltic Sea network. Joint projects are being conducted, for example, in the field of analytical measuring methods, the production of medicines and vaccines, and the development and implementation of hygiene standards.

Internet tip:
www.bcv.org

Chalk line separates Sassnitz from Lenin

Seaport was gateway to Russian revolutionaries' homeland

After the 1917 February Revolution in Russia multinational Bolsheviks, having lived in exile in neutral Switzerland, headed homewards with a view to disempowering the old regime.

From Zurich, the party which included Vladimir Ilyich Ulyanov – named Lenin – planned their route in detail. They planned to pass the Swiss-German border at Gottmadingen. Their journey lead from Berne in Switzerland via Stuttgart, Frankfurt and Berlin to the north easternmost corner of Germany. The travellers had been assured unperturbed transit by the German government in order to weaken the Russian enemy. From Sassnitz they intended to

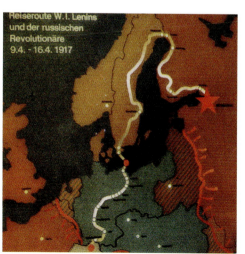

A map in the former Lenin Memorial in Sassnitz showed the route taken by the revolutionaries.

take a ferry to Trelleborg. From there, the journey was to be continued via Stockholm and Tornea to native St. Petersburg.

On 9th April, 1917, the travellers entered the express train No. 263 in Bern and later stopped in Gottmadingen. On arriving at the German border, the emigrants hoped for an unproblematic change of trains. Officers, however, lead the party into the waiting room where they spent several anxious minutes. But no passport control. Relieved, the travellers boarded the next train – or rather a wagon divided into eight passenger and one luggage compartment. Thus, Lenin was intented on protecting his fellows from German contact. Fortunately, German frontier guards abided by the agreement. In Gottmadingen, the travellers boarded a different train accompanied by two military officers as escort. While on German territory, no one was allowed outside the train. To assure their protection and to distinguish Russian territory, a white chalk line was drawn on the train floor. One end of the carriage was allocated to the revolutionaries, the other to the German officers. Furthermore, the external doors to the train were locked.

On 12th April in the early evening, the sealed train arrived safely in Sassnitz. Many excited citizens awaited its arrival, but met with disappointment when none of the expected Russian aristocrats departed from the carriage. The islanders drew back – very much suiting Lenin's plans of remaining unrecognised.

He and his party spent the night inside the train, still protected by armed officers. Early the next morning they embarked the ferry. Again, the emigrants had to endure several anxious minutes: the Swedish authorities de-

Internet tip:
www.sassnitz.de

In this wagon visitors could follow the wake of Lenin.

manded a passenger list before anyone was allowed to board. Confidently, the revolutionaries entered false names and finally passed up the gangway of the "Drottning Victoria" to take them homewards. Having spent almost ten years in exile, Lenin and the revolutionaries arrived in St. Petersburg on 16th April 1917. At home, the carriers of hope were greeted by a crowd and by a guard of honour at Finland Station. Lenin is said to have climbed a tank in order to appeal to the public to support the revolution.

Until 1990, an exceptional memorial used to remind of Lenin's journey. A green railway wagon similar to the one that carried the party to Sassnitz, housed a Lenin exhibition. A compartment equipped with Lenin's utensils invited visitors to an exciting journey through time.

Further reading:
Pearson, M.
The sealed train, New York 1975.

Relatively famous honorary doctor

Rostock University dignified Albert Einstein

The University of Rostock was the only university in the whole of Germany that honoured the genius of the twentieth century, Albert Einstein (1879-1955), by awarding him an honorary doctorate. The Rostock alma mater is among the many institutions of higher education, such as those of Geneva, Princeton, Oxford and Zurich, which recognised the great physicist in this way. Curiously, he was honoured by the Faculty of Medicine.

Moritz Schlick, who taught at the University of Rostock from 1910 until 1921 and at whose home Einstein was a frequent visitor, had advocated the bestowal of an honorary doctorate on him. Evidently, it was not the Faculty of Mathematics and the Natural Sciences that supported this proposal, but rather the Faculty of Medicine. As well as Einstein, other scientists including Max Planck were awarded the honorary doctorate on the occasion of the University's 500th anniversary on 12th November 1919.

Einstein had qualified as a teacher of mathematics and physics in Zurich at the age of 21. In 1905, the publication of his work on the theory of relativity he expanded the foundations of physics and mathematics. At the age of 29, he worked as a lecturer at the University of Berne. He became a member of the Prussian Academy of Sciences in 1913 and headed the newly founded Kaiser Wilhelm Institute of Physics in Berlin later.

Einstein's theory of relativity was initially disputed in scientific circles. Particularly in Germany, his genius was not immediately recognised. However, measurements of renowned astronomers during the solar eclipse that occurred on 29th May of the same year confirmed Einstein's calculations and he became world famous.

Albert Einstein was awarded the Nobel Prize for Physics in Stockholm in 1922, the Copley Medal of the Royal Society of London in 1925, the Gold Medal of the Royal Astronomical Society in 1926 and the Benjamin Franklin Medal in Philadelphia in 1935. During the course of his life the brilliant physicist was granted more than 25 honorary doctorates. The famous scientist travelled extensively in Europe and South America and emigrated to the USA in 1933. He evidently held fond memories of the Hanseatic city on the Baltic coast. In a thank-you letter to the University he wrote, "The sincere hospitality that was shown to me in Rostock will always remain a pleasant memory for me." Incidentally, Einstein liked Mecklenburg and Western Pomerania so much that he spent his summer holidays at the Baltic coast several times. In Sellin, Ahrenshoop, Wustrow and Ribnitz he enjoyed and appreciated the "...absolute peace".

This portrait was made in 1951 at a party celebrating Albert Einstein's birthday.

Internet tip:
www.alberteinstein.info

Pomeranian man battles his way through

Max Schmeling maintains links to his birthplace

He fought his way right to the top – in every class! The World Professional Boxing champion Max Schmeling (1905-2005) was born in the hamlet of Klein Luckow near Pasewalk.

He bore the title of world heavyweight champion from 1930 to 1932. In 70 professional fights, he achieved 56 victories and suffered ten defeats. Four times, he left the ring after a drawn fight.

Champion Schmeling hit the headlines in 1936, when he defeated the "Brown Bomber", Joe Louis, in the ring. The American was considered invincible, but the man from Western Pomerania hit him so hard in the twelfth round that he went down. A sensational success for "Maxe"! The Nazi regime misused his success for propaganda purposes. In private, however, there were no power struggles between the combatants. On the contrary: they were firm friends. Louis outclassed Schmeling in the return match, but the sportsmen kept in contact. In fact, the German professional later even supported his American friend financially – even beyond his death: when Louis died in 1981, Schmeling bore part of the costs of the funeral.

Schmeling ended his active career in 1948. His sporting ambition and an American friend soon revived the boxer's fortunes, however, and he

In his active period Max Schmeling was able to chalk up 56 boxing victories.

operated in Hamburg as the general representative in North Germany for products of the Coca-Cola group. The decency, compassion and modesty which he maintained during and after his career made him a global legend in his lifetime.

The gentle fist fighter felt attached not only to his ring opponents, but also to his native place. The Max-Schmeling foundation finances a carer job in the parish of Blumenhagen – even after his death. A woman still supplies the wants of needy people in the region today from the support of the boxing legend.

The Pomeranian village of Klein Luckow laid a memorial stone to its freeman Schmeling on the occasion of his 101st birthday on 28th September 2006. The boxer battled his way to a championship title outside the ring too – in his homeland and in America – with his social commitment and fair play.

Internet tip:
www.boxinggyms.com

Following his boxing career, Schmeling worked periodically as a representative for the Coca-Cola concern in North Germany.

Trans-Siberian departs at Sassnitz harbour

Rügen port is station of the world's longest railway line

Germany's largest island Rügen can proudly claim to be the location of the most efficient train ferry harbour at the Baltic Sea and thus the gate to Scandinavia and the Baltic. The harbour is also known as the "westernmost cargo station of the Trans-Siberian railway". At first glance Russia's main traffic axis seems to be too far away to be related to the Sassnitz ferry harbour. But it is the only port location of Western Europe offering track and trans-shipment facilities for rail cars of the Russian broad gauge. This qualifies the island of Rügen as an international handling junction.

The port in Sassnitz offers modern facilities for passenger traffic and cargo handling.

During the past few years the port of Sassnitz, situated on the north east side of the Isle of Rügen, was upgraded and enlarged for freight and passengers to reach their destinations in Sweden, Russia and the Baltic states as fast as possible. After just 3 hours, for example, advanced ships, so called combi ro-pax ferries, tie up at Trelleborg.

Besides cargo ships and ferries, more and more cruise ships are anchored at Sassnitz port. The appealing harbour terminal proves to be as comfortable as the giant hotels of the sea themselves. Equipped with modern facilities, Mukran is gaining importance as a harbour that cruise liners and club cruisers call at.

Internet tips:
www.faehrhafen-sassnitz.de
www.sassnitz.de
www.transsib.de

Hairy immigrants from China

Fishermen find exotic sea dwellers

Mecklenburg-Western Pomerania welcomes inflow from all over the world – and not only onshore. On top of all the visiting students, immigrants, tourists and foreign workers, a shaggy crustacean from the Far East also made its home in our federal state. Chinese mitten crabs made their way to the Elbe as early as the start of the last century. They started their long journey form Asia in the ballast water of the merchant ships.

The crabs were initially far from welcome among the local fishermen. The brown omnivores have almost no natural enemies and threatened the local fauna and also effortlessly cut through the nets of the annoyed fishermen. Recently, however, the exotic creatures have begun to be marketed as delicacies.

The company Binnenfischerei Mecklenburg GmbH in Dömitz, for instance, supplements its summer business by marketing the crustaceans. Asian restaurants and shops buy the crabs. In Asia the crustacean is a speciality – prepared like lobster or in soup.

Now and then by the way, the hairy crabs can also be admired at the Stralsund Museum of Oceanography. The last specimens have, however, recently escaped from the aquarium. The Chinese immigrants are such skilful scramblers that they find an exit out of almost every tank.

Deutsches
Meeresmuseum
Katharinenberg 14
18439 Stralsund
Tel. +49(0)3831
2650210

Internet tips:
www.bimes.de
www.meeres-museum.de

Indian Sherlock Holmes from Teterow

Farmer's son became commissioner of police

Robert H. Vincent periodically also fought for Guiseppe Garibaldi.

The way for a gifted Mecklenburg man in the mid 19th century led to India. The ambitious Robert Hampe Vincent rendered outstanding services to police security in Mumbai. Vincent sees the light of day near Teterow, in the heart of Mecklenburg, in 1841. At first the farmer's son wants to do a trader apprenticeship in Magdeburg, but he soon finds the cramped little shop unbearable. He leaves his homeland for Italy, where he attaches himself to Giuseppe Garibaldi's legendary movement to create an Italian state. After being wounded and imprisoned, however, he quits and heads for England as a sailor, where he is hired on a cargo ship bound for the British colony India. Hooked by the culture and people, Robert Vincent stays and exerts himself all over the country to find a situation. On walkabout again, this time on the subcontinent, he studies the alien culture. In his thirst for knowledge, the Mecklenburger learns here 30 of the myriad different languages of the Indian people. His drive and ability bring him a job offer from the police after seven years with the military.

He starts a remarkable career. On 8th April 1893, after only a few years' service, Robert Vincent becomes Commissioner of Police of the city of Bombay. Supported by the British colonial government he restructures the security forces in order to increase their clout. Soon there are 2,500 policemen deployed in Bombay and the man from Mecklenburg achieves major successes in fighting crime through the introduction of new methods such as examining fingerprints.

Bombay was marked by severe conflicts in the 19th century.

In the Bombay of the 19th century, the police are not merely confronted with commonplace conflicts. Violent clashes between Hindus and Muslims and protests against the colonial government require the utmost of the guardians of order. It rapidly becomes clear to Vincent that his men are not up to the task of dealing with these battles and he does not hesitate to demand military aid to avoid worse befalling. And during the cholera epidemic of 1896, Vincent manages to keep the numbers of looters and burglars low. The Mecklenburg man retires at the start of 1899 and receives numerous commendations for his services in fighting criminality. As a mark of his great recognition he is assigned yet one more high office in his well-earned retirement: Vincent becomes chairman of the city council and gets the task of reforming the Egyptian police for good measure. When he demands dramatic hygienic measures in a new cholera epidemic, however, he comes up against protest on the part of the government. Embittered, he resigns his office. His love for India however remains and, with his wife, he undertakes a journey through the entire country, which the government underwrites.

The remarkable man of Mecklenburg never returns to his homeland, even though to Europe: he dies on 12th October 1914 in Lugano.

First white man on Easter Island

Rostocker discovered Pacific island

Internet tip:
www.metmuseum.org

Gigantic stone images with huge noses and much too small bodies doubtless sent shivers up the spines of Carl Friedrich Behrens. At second glance, however, the colossal faces actually look quite friendly and aroused the curiosity of the first white man stepping on Easter Island. The son of an old Rostock mariner family went ashore from the ship of the Dutch Admiral Roggeveen, which moored before the coast of the Pacific island on its search for Australia.

The adventuresome Behrens had signed on as a sort of warrant officer. After exploring Königsberg and St. Petersburg, he had strayed into Swedish captivity before Danzig and had escaped. The 21-year-old globetrotter set course in 1722 with the expedition of Admiral Roggeveen for Tierra del Fuego.

He had already been drawn away to distant countries as a 13-year-old, explained the Rostock man in his book "Der wohlversuchte Sued-Laender", which was published in 1738 and turned out to be a bestseller of its time. In his description of the voyage, he proudly related being the first white man to dare to go on shore between the stone colossi on Easter Sunday 1722. The island of Rapa Nui entered the history books as Easter Island and, after Behrens, many scientists researched the moais, those enigmatic cult figures, which still line the beach of the island today.

Strelitz woman on the throne of the Empire

Charlotte of Mecklenburg-Strelitz married George III

Queen Victoria's grandmother, the later monarch Sophie Charlotte, came from Mecklenburg. She was born on 19th May, 1744 in the tiny German town of Mirow. Seventeen years later, no less a person than the King of England, George III of the House of Hanover, asked for her hand. He is said to have been impressed by both her beauty and her intelligence. They then married on 8th September 1761 in St. James Palace in London.

Four days later, Sophie Charlotte was crowned Queen of the Empire, but on the condition that she was not to involve herself in politics. Thus, Queen Charlotte totally devoted herself to her family. She gave birth to fifteen children, nine sons and six daughters. She was interested in literature and music, and her versatility enhanced her popularity with her people. She was so popular, that emigrants settling in America named their new home town Charlotte in honour of their Mecklenburg Queen in 1763.

The reigning couple's marriage was a harmonious one. Both particularly liked country life. They most favoured residing at Kew Palace, south east of London, right in the middle of a tremendous park. One of the Queen's greatest interests lay in the creative expansion and sup-

Queen Charlotte around 1765

www.sayers-strelitzia.com.au

port of the Royal botanical gardens at Kew. Even to this day, people are invited to visit the summer residence of "Queen Charlotte's Cottage", hidden among the high trees of Kew Park that Queen Charlotte was given when she got married. Today, the Royal Botanic Gardens at Kew are a Unesco World heritage site and renowned for being some of the most beautiful gardens in Great Britain. The strelitzia reginae was declared the official flower of the Mecklenburg town of Neustrelitz. Certainly, it will play an important role during the celebrations of the 250th anniversary of Charlotte's coronation in 2011.

Being a monarch during the Enlightenment, King George encouraged and supported many scientists and explorers to collect exotic plants in England's many colonies and bring them back to London. In 1772, Francis Masson joined James Cook for his journey to South Africa. At the Cape of Good Hope, he collected a very special plant, a crane lily, better known as "Bird of Paradise Flower". His orderer, the famous natural scientist Joseph Banks, named the plant "Strelitzia Reginae" in honour of his Queen.

Mozart's music for Mecklenburg's monarchs

Genius composed for Strelitz Dukes

Vienna and Salzburg are the places most closely associated with the legendary composer. However, Wolfgang Amadeus Mozart's path also crossed that of the nobility of Mecklenburg. Princess Sophie Charlotte of Mecklenburg-Strelitz, met the musical genius for the first time after she had become Queen of Great Britain and Ireland. The German composer Leopold Mozart came to the British royal court in April 1764 in order to present his highly gifted children, Amadeus and Nannerl. Queen Sophie Charlotte, who was known for her open-mindedness, invited the children to give a private performance the very next day. Since the granting of such a personal meeting so soon was quite exceptional, a friendly relationship quickly developed between the Mozart family and the British court. Mozart dedicated six sonatas for piano and flute (KV 10-15) to Sophie Charlotte.

He honoured not only the British Queen but also Duke Georg August of Mecklenburg-Strelitz (1748-1785) with a piece of music. At the joint memorial service for him and his fellow freemason Count Franz Esterhazy on 17th November 1785, Mozart's Masonic Funeral Music (KV 477) was performed at the Vienna Freemasons' lodge. This piece is regarded as an occasional composition of highest rank.

Internet tip:
www.mozart.at

Mozart Nights like this one in Güstrow recall times gone by.

Stormy petrel on the sun island

Maxim Gorky recuperates in Usedom's bracing climate

"Ku'damm in front, Baltic Sea behind" quipped Kurt Tucholsky about the "bathtub of the Berliners". What he meant is the sun island Usedom, which attracted not just the locals in the age of the Kaiser. Among the most famous spa guests seeking healing in the mild sea climate was Maxim Gorky. The Russian writer and "stormy petrel of the revolution" came with his son, the latter's wife and a friend to Heringsdorf in May 1921. He stayed at the Villa Irmgard, the position of which he found pleasantly undisturbed. Gorky was hoping for recovery from his tuberculosis and enjoyed the beach, sea and wind on long morning walks on the island. He was soon accompanied on these rambles by a faithful fellow countryman and like-minded person: Leo Tolstoy. Long conversations about homeland and literature are

Villa "Irmgard" in Heringsdorf

supposed to have played their part in causing Tolstoy later to return to Russia. The famous opera singer and friend of Gorky, Fyodor Chaliapin, also attached himself to the constructive talks of the artists on Usedom from time to time.

Sun, beach and sea also inspired the man of letters to the first version of the third part of his autobiography "My Universities". Despite his recuperation, the miserable conditions on the Usedom of the twenties did not escape the critical Gorky. The children of the poor begged in the so-called Kaiserbäder (imperial spas) too – a situation which Gorky dealt with in his sketch "The Colony of the Bedraggled".

Maxim Gorky left his place of recuperation on 25th September 1922 – what have remained are his name and silent witnesses, which can still be viewed today at the Villa Irmgard. The neoclassical villa receives visitors in rooms appointed in the style of that period. Today's Museum of Regional and Literary History revives the past with special exhibitions, book readings, concerts and plays.

Internet tips:
www.mvweb.de
www.drei-kaiserbaeder.de

Museum
Villa «Irmgard»
Maxim-Gorki-Straße 13
17424 Heringsdorf
Tel. +49(0)38378 22361

Looking for a homeland

Writer Uwe Johnson remained devoted to Mecklenburg

"Where I in truth belong is the densely wooded Mecklenburg lake district from Plau to Templin", was how the writer Uwe Johnson summed himself up. However, he came to be on a lifelong search for a home, of a spiritual rather than a geographical nature. Born in Pomeranian Cammin, he grew up in Mecklenburg, and the land and the people won his heart. However, he left Mecklenburg because of irreconcilable differences with the state apparatus of the GDR. In 1959, "Mutmassungen über Jacob" was published by the West German Suhrkamp publishing house, which Johnson took as an occasion to move to the West. The fate of the character Jacob Abs has since found acclaim beyond the borders of Germany. Readers in many European countries, and even Korea and Japan, have followed and continue to follow Johnson's reflexion of German-German history.

Likewise dissatisfied with conditions in the western part of Germany, he took the opportunity in 1966 of becoming acquainted with the metropolis of New York – and stayed. He spent two years in the "Big Apple", first as a textbook editor and later as a stipendiary of the Rockefeller Foundation. He found countryside and coastal scenery around New York that reminded him of that of home.

In 1968, in America, he started to write his main work "Jahrestage. Aus dem Leben von Gesine Cresspahl". The problems of being uprooted,

Literaturhaus
»Uwe Johnson«
Im Thurow 14
23948 Klütz
Tel. +49(0)38825 22387

equally applicable to many other people in wartime and post-war Germany, are demonstrated by Johnson in the example of Gesine Cresspahl. With the American edition "Anniversaries", Johnson confronted American readers too with German-German history.

In Germany Johnson was showered with honours. He was awarded several literary prizes and was Vice President of the Academy of Arts in West Berlin from 1972 to 1974. But all these successes did not allow Johnson to find a home in West Germany. In 1974 he moved to England, to the Isle of Sheppey on the Thames. Here too, Johnson surrounded himself with memories of the homeland. A large map of Mecklenburg decorated a wall in his house in Sheerness-on-Sea, for example. In a kind of declaration of love, Johnson immortalised the people, scenery and history of Mecklenburg-Western Pomerania in his works. Shortly before his death in 1984, his fellow writer Max Frisch remarked: "This man has a Homeric memory. Mecklenburg can rely on that."

Uwe Johnson in autumn of 1981

Greifswalder surveys giant waterfall

Development worker explores attraction in virgin forest

Angry water masses plunge into the deeps – several million litres a second, amazing 771 metres.

This natural spectacle was long hidden from the world. It was only in March 2006 that the Greifswalder Stefan Ziemendorff led a camera team into the Peruvian forest to allow the public to participate in his fantastic discovery. The development worker and hobby archaeologist had already come across the enormous Gocta waterfall in 2002. He made his way through the pathless rain forest to the legendary cataract, with the support of a German-Peruvian team. In the course of three expeditions, they discovered that the cataract relegated the third-highest natural spectacle of this kind in Yosemite (USA) to fourth place. The now world famous waterfall is named after the nearby village in the Peruvian province of Chachapoyas.

There is believed to be a treasure of gold at the Gocta.

For the inhabitants, however, the natural spectacle is rather uncanny. That explains why the Gocta Falls were not marked on any map for so long. According to legend, a blond beauty lives in their wild waters, a siren, and a fearsome serpent. As the mother of the fish of the river, the siren does not just watch over the nature, but also protects a fabulous gold hoard. So she is supposed to have execrated the Indian Juan

Mendoza for coming too close to her treasure. Now, as punishment, he ekes out his days as a rock, with the torrential floods thundering unceasingly over his shoulders into the depths. Severe and silent, decorative figures of ancient sarcophagi observe proceedings from the opposite side.

Visitors and tourists have not only been deterred from marvelling at the waterfall by superstition. The virtually impassable nature has also played its part. The dense, almost untouched rain forest all makes any approach extremely difficult. All the more do wonderful animal species make this their habitat. Spectacled bears, pumas, toucans and other animals threatened with extinction have remained undisturbed in the 3,300 square kilometre nature reserve up to now. This paradise is, however, currently threatened by extensive agriculture. Stefan Ziemendorff places his hopes, as do many inhabitants of Cocachimba, on tourism as a less destructive source of income.

He was one of the first adventurers to dare to penetrate so far into the pathless region. He was guided and accompanied by the 60 year old native Telesforo Santillan, who likewise turned back shortly before the watery monster and left Ziemendorff alone with his tent and equipment.

The development worker had discovered Peru during an intern at the international humanitarian aid, and it so fascinated him that he stayed. Today, Stefan Ziemendorff is adviser to the water distribution company and is involved as coordinator with the project 100,000 water and wastewater connections. His interest in archaeology has drawn him repeatedly to the waterfall region.

> Higher than the now measured waterfall are only Salto Angel in Venezuela at 972 and Tugela Falls in South Africa at 948 metres.

Wismar car in Olso museum

Technical Museum houses only preserved Mecklenburg automobile

Internet tip:
www.visitoslo.com

Connoisseurs dug out a real treasure in a Norwegian barn in 1963: a rusty beauty, 51 years of age. The old wreck found not just turned out to be very old; in fact, it is the only preserved car ever built in Mecklenburg-Western Pomerania.

The car had been fabricated by the industrial magnate Heinrich Podeus (1832-1905). The tycoon had established international reputation importing coal and constructing agricultural and marine machines, waggons and – last but not least – cars. Several state-of-the-art models left the Wismar Podeus garage. Mecklenburg technicians kept up with the times: padded leather seats, folding top, and first class wooden spokewheels indulged their drivers in luxury. Podeus' cars turned out to be real export hits. Even Argentina proved to be mightily impressed by Wismar limousines and roadsters.

The Podeus car drove through Wismar one more time in 1997.

The car found in the Norwegian barn had been used as a taxi by its first owner. Nowadays, almost a century later, the ever shining 94-year-old oldtimer carrying the registration number A:5422 is displayed in the Oslo Technical Museum.

In 1997, the real Podeus car went back home to Wismar and took part in the First Ostfold-Wismar-Oldtimer-Rallye.

From the Müritz all over the seas

Waren propeller manufacturer leads global market

The famous luxury liner QUEEN MARY II, which sails around the world under the British flag, would not make any headway at all without its huge propellers. Four of them propel the floating palace. An amazing 140,000 hp are transmitted over the enormous propellers to move the longest sea hotel in the world forwards. The giant propellers were produced in the middle of Mecklenburg-Western Pomerania. Mecklenburger Metallguss GmbH is based in Waren on the Müritz lake and manufactures propellers for all categories and sizes of ship. The record propeller has an incredible 9.60 metre bore diameter and weighs 135 tonnes; its drive horse power is 120,000.

The MMG GmbH works has been making a noise for more than a century. It was founded at its present location as "Maschinenfabrik and Eisengiesserei" (engineering works and iron foundry) in the year 1875. Since the 1940's the company has specialised in producing propellers. MMG exports roughly 80 per cent of the propellers manufactured to companies around the world.

Internet tip:
www.mmg-propeller.de

The Mecklenburg company has been cultivating contacts with the major South Korean shipyards Samsung Heavy Industries, Daewoo Shipbuilding and Hanjin Heavy Industries. The fastest container ship in the world, built by Daewoo Shipbuilding, is driven by an MMG propeller. The Waren company also supplied the propeller for the MSC PAMELA, the largest container ship in the world. At a bore of 8.80 metres, this colossus weighs 93 tonnes.

The second largest partner of the Metallguss factory after South Korea is China. Beside the Asian partners, the French shipyard Chantiers de l'Atlantique and the well-known Italian

Gigantic propellers find their way from Waren to the water.

shipbuilding company Fincantieri have been associates of the company for seven years. Other customers of the propeller manufacturer are shipyards in Denmark, Poland, Portugal, Cro-atia, Brazil, Indonesia, India and numerous shipping companies.

Mecklenburger Metallguss GmbH manufactures internationally valued products. This is ensured by ultra-modern furnaces and the highest engineering standards, which allow the propellers to be manufactured in environmentally friendly fashion.

High-precision propeller boring and milling machines process propellers with a bore of up to 11.3 metres with a precision of a few hundredths of a millimetre. But despite the state-of-the-art engineering, no propeller is perfect without the fine honing of the experienced Metallguss employees. Highly sensitive areas are still ground by hand.

Regatta network across the Baltic

Baltic Sail marks the maritime summer-highlight

A layperson can rapidly lose their bearings with so many sailing events: Baltic or Hanse Sail, sailing festivals, Marine and Sea Festival. But one thing they all have in common: the Baltic Sea. Young and old, professional and recreational seadogs cordially invite interested parties every summer, to sniff the fresh Baltic Sea air from a windjammer, as did once the legendary Klaus Störtebeker, – and not just in Mecklenburg-Western Pomerania, but internationally. The cities of Rostock, Karlkrona, Gdansk, Helsingør, Lübeck, Halmstad and Klaipeda have joined forces under the name Baltic Sail and allowed their museum ships, traditional and large sailing vessels moor at the Baltic ports.

In 1996, the Hanseatic city of Rostock seized the initiative in setting up this association. Innumerable ships cruise the Baltic Sea during the Baltic Sail each July and August.

Internet tips:
www.baltic-sail.com
www.hanse-sail.com

Many visitors are attracted to Rostock by the Hanse Sail every year.

Sun King's traces in Schwerin Lake

Grand Duke erected palace following French model

Internet tip:
www.schwerin.com

C'est fantastique! Splendid festivals in a scenery just like at court of Louis XIV – Mecklenburg's dukes also celebrated them in Schwerin. Architects created a fairytale castle upon the pattern of the renaissance château of Chambord, right in the heart of France, at the ducal residence of Schwerin.

Grand Duke Frederik Francis II planned to built a castle amidst the Schwerin Lake after the court had returned from Ludwigslust residence in 1837. The palace was meant to stand at the site of the former island castle "Zuarin" of prince Niclot of the Obotrites that had burned down in 1160. Gottfried Semper, well known for the Dresden Opera, designed a new magnificent building incorporating stylistic devices from the Renaissance. He recreated many elements of Loire châteaus combining them with gables and arches. Sempers plan was abolished in the end, for he had disregarded the little scope of the Schwerin Lake island the castle was to be built on. Still, his ideas remained. The architects Demmler and Willebrand, instructed by the Grand Duke to complete the work, collected impulses in France, England and Southern Germany in 1844. Back home, they formulated a new concept following the architecture of the biggest castle of the Loir region: Château Chambord. Finally, the Duke and his family settled in their new – international – fairytale palace in May

1857. After many conceptions and as many foremen the architects succeeded in creating a 19th century renaissance building, whose golden dome gleams with royal élégance within Schwerin's skyline still today.

But not only Schwerin Castle invites its visitors to a round-the-world trip. Carl-Joseph Lenné also set out an English garden surrounding the

Schwerin Castle was given its fairy-tale appearance in the 19th century.

palace and thus enriched the park creating international flair. Groves from all over the world may still be admired today. Mediterranean atmosphere also awaits Schwerin visitors, who will be delighted by the gorgeous view off the restored orangery through arches and fountains towards the deep blue of Schwerin Lake. Incidentally, Schwerin Castle still houses the government. The Mecklenburg-Western Pomeranian legislative assembly has its seat in the fairytale palace with a French touch.

Romanov residence near Rostock

High nobility family reunion at the Baltic Sea

Internet tip:
www.jsgelbensande.de

Roofed stairs of the hunting manor.

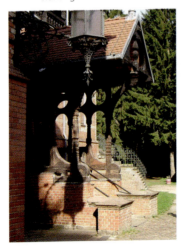

Among its high firs, the heath near Rostock mysteriously hides a charming jewel. Apparelled with many turrets and gables, the pretty mansion made of brick reminds of an ancient Russian fairytale. Indeed, the hunting lodge of Gelbensande often received visitors from Russia.

Grand Duke of Mecklenburg-Schwerin Friedrich Franz III (1851-1897) and his wife Anastasia, Her Imperial Highness Grand Duchess of Russia, chose the woodland scenery by the Baltic Sea as perfect location to erect their summer residence. Master builder Gotthilf Ludwig Möckel had been commissioned by Friedrich Franz III to edify the manor house.

No less a person than the son of the Russian Tsar himself, Michail Nikolajewitsch Romanov, generously participated in financing the manor house. Thus, not quite unselfishly, the Russian grand duke and father of Anastasia, gained the right to reside in Gelbensande. Every once in a while, he made use of his privilege to recover from government business in the healthy maritime climate. Also, the stylish gabled roof on top of the outside stairs is said to have been set up at Romanov's explicit desire, because he was used to reach his pompous coach without touching muddy ground.

To make the Russian grand prince and his daughter feel at home, architect Möckel enriched the hunting lodge by many ornamentations similar to those of Russian manor houses. Besides, he placed the heraldic animal of the Russian eagle in different parts of the building.

Still today, people of noble birth visit the lodge to marvel at their ancestor's beautiful residence. The current Prince Consort Henrik of Denmark, for example, visited it in July 2002. Wearing a casual shirt and sandals, he wandered through the hall, the lounge, the kitchen and the park, very keen on learning about his wife's ancestors. Queen Margaret, reigning monarch of Denmark, is granddaughter of Alexandrine, who got married to Christian X, Crown Prince of Denmark in April 1898.

After the Grand Duke's death, Duchess and landlady Anastasia resided at Gelbensande for a while. From 1914, however, she preferred the Mediterranean climate of Cannes in France, where the royal family owned another villa. Grand Duke Friedrich Franz IV and his family made use of the castle as a principal domicile then. Later, the residence was used as a sickbay and a hospital.

Since 1995 an association has restored and maintaind Gelbensande castle and welcomes about 20,000 visitors to the museum each year. In the faithfully restored dining room concerts and events take place. Lovers, more than 100 couples a year, enjoy the special atmosphere getting married in the castle.

> Förderverein
> Jagdschloss
> Gelbensande e. V.
> Am Schloss 1
> 18182 Gelbensande
> Tel. +49(0)038201 475

The whole alphabet on seven keys

Pasewalker invents a typewriter for the blind

Oskar Picht, a teacher from Pasewalk, invented a somewhat different kind of typewriter. The special thing about it was that it had only seven large keys. Nevertheless, the whole alphabet and all the numbers could be written on it. Picht invented the machine to make learning easier for his visually impaired pupils. The keys are pressed simultaneously in different combinations to punch little raised dots into paper. Successor models are still in use today, from Argentina to Taiwan.

Internet tip:
www.erikapicht.de

Picht based his invention on the system of writing developed in 1825 by the Frenchman Louis Braille. Six dots are arranged in three rows of two to form a basic character or cell. For each letter, certain points are omitted, with each of the patterns so produced standing for a different letter. By means of this system, Braille enabled many non-sighted people to read and write. However, writing was quite difficult, as all the dots had to be impressed individually into the paper with the aid of a table. Also, the pupils had to write from right to left in order to be able to read from left to right, because the paper had to be turned over to feel the raised dots.

Oskar Picht made working with the visually impaired the central focus of his life. In 1899 he became a teacher at the School for the Blind in Berlin-Steglitz, of which he later became head

A modern version of the "Erika-Picht" is still sold today around the world.

teacher. Unfortunately, the school library was sparsely equipped and few printing companies produced expensive books in Braille. This dilemma inspired Picht to develop a machine that could make writing in Braille quick and easy. His invention gained world renown in 1899, even though he was not the only person to have created a Braille writing machine. In America, the device known as the Perkins Brailler had also been invented. At the International Typewriter Exhibition in Venice in 1907, however, it was Picht who was granted the highest award, the gold medal. Six years earlier, he had obtained the first patent, and he gained nine more for further improvements. Picht increased the stocks of the school library, which soon grew into one of the largest lending libraries in Germany.

His typewriter later became a highly successful export, marketed under the name "Erika-Picht". It is still being sold by multi-tech GmbH in Dresden to customers all over the world, from America to the Far East.

Picht's hometown of Pasewalk has called the local school after this dedicated teacher and each year awards the Oskar Picht Prize for special achievements at school and in extracurricular activities.

A modern surgeon

Christian Theodor Billroth operated throughout the world

"Scalpel please!" Some assistants of Christian Theodor Billroth may well have felt queasy on this command. In the times of the innovative surgeon, some of his techniques by no means formed part of the daily operation routine. The father of gastrointestinal surgery ranks among the most important surgeons of the 19th century and was in some regards ahead of his time.

The gifted doctor was born in Bergen on the Isle of Rügen in 1829. After his studies at the universities of Greifswald, Göttingen and Berlin, he opened new ways to healing for his patients.

With plastic surgery skills and a doctorate, Billroth followed an appointment as Director to the Clinic of Surgery in Zurich in 1859. He passed on his knowledge at the Swiss university and often studied into the night and nevertheless devoted himself with new findings to everyday hospital life from seven in the morning. He published numerous scientific works from the city on the Limmat, which, in foreign language editions as well, conquered the world. He discovered the streptococci, promoted hospital and nursing care and founded the Rudolfiner house of nursing training. From 1867 the doctor also researched in the Austrian capital. His results in gastrointestinal surgery represent the highlight of his career. In 1881, he introduced new scientific procedures

Stadtmuseum von Bergen
Im Klosterhof
18528 Bergen
Tel. +49(0)3838 252226

with his operation methods, called, after him, "Billroth I and II", thus saving the lives of innumerable cancer patients.

Young doctors and students streamed to his lecture hall from all points of the compass. People in Athens, Naples, Constantinople, Paris, Lisbon and St. Petersburg sent for the famous surgeon. Billroth was a member of seventy scientific societies at home and abroad. Still during his lifetime, a plaque was put up on his birthplace to the "outstanding surgeon of his age". His home town Bergen later named the entire street after the demigod in white. Today, the town museum in Bergen monastery yard remembers the groundbreaking triumphs of the gifted surgeon and interested visitors can explore his roots during a Billroth walking tour through his home town.

Christian Theodor Billroth developed modern methods of surgery.

Victuals for Lord Nelson

Warnemünde received
important visitors

On Whit Sunday 1801, countless citizens of Warnemünde and Rostock thronged the quayside of the Baltic Sea resort. No less a personage than the English Admiral Nelson was honouring them with his presence at the mouth of the Warnow. From the warship St. George, which carried 120 cannons, the sailor commanded the English fleet, which after its successful naval battle before Copenhagen was now anchored before Warnemünde. The Englishmen recovered for a full two weeks before the Baltic Sea resort from the exertions of the war at sea and the people of Mecklenburg flocked to Warnemünde in order not to miss the unusual spectacle. The Duke of Mecklenburg-Strelitz himself, Karl Ludwig Friedrich, did not miss the opportunity of visiting the fleet on 1st June. After all, a few years previously, he had been the closest confidant of the British Queen, his sister Sophie Charlotte. The British crews welcomed him with saluting fire and parades.

This view of Warnemünde from the sea was made in 1825.

After naval hero Nelson and his men had stocked up on supplies of fresh water and victuals and recovered from the battle, they left the hospitable harbour of Warnemünde on 8th June 1801.

Mecklenburger found ancient clay tablets in Palestine

Ernst Sellin excavated Jericho

Ernst Sellin (1867-1904) is not only a figurehead for universities in Mecklenburg, but was also awarded an honorary doctorate from St. Andrews University in Scotland.

Born in Altschwerin/Mecklenburg, Ernst Sellin made a distinguished career. After completing his high school diploma in Ratzeburg in 1884, he studied Oriental languages and theology in Rostock, as well as in Erlangen and Leipzig. After his dissertation in he taught as a secondary school teacher in Parchim.

In 1897 he went to the University of Vienna in order to obtain his doctorate, and in 1908 returned to his Alma mater in Rostock as a professor of Old Testament exegesis and archaeology.

Again and again, however, the Mecklenburger journeyed to the far edges of the world. Ruins in Palestine's Tannach were excavated under his direction between 1902 and 1904. His discoveries there awarded him the undivided attention of science. He is credited with the excavation of the only known clay tablets inscribed with wedges dating back more than 3,500 years. Moreover, Sellin planned the exploration of the legendary city of Jericho in Palestine. With the support of the German Oriental Society he, together with Carl Watzinger, was able to carry out the excavations between 1907 and 1909. The excavations reached back until 1500 B.C. and were the greatest success of Sellin's career.

Captivated by the Dark Continent

Paul Pogge advanced from big game hunter to Africanist

Goods, money, social recognition – Paul Pogge left all his prosperity in Mecklenburg behind to dedicate himself to exploring Africa. Driven at first by a sheer desire to hunt, the adventurer turned into a plant collector, cartographer, and cultural missionary.

In 1864, the explorer started out the first time for South Africa, in order to take part in a big game hunt. In 1874, he joined an expedition of the ornithologist and entomologist Alexander von Homeyer, which aimed to open up trade routes into the south of the present-day Republic of Congo. His companions, however, became seriously ill so, in 1875, Pogge moved by himself into the residence of the African prince Muata Jamwo. From here he undertook day trips and travelled the Congo basin. When he returned to Germany in 1877, he had extensive material in his luggage. The success of his travels found recognition not only in Germany, but in England, France and Belgium as well. His precious collection of 400 species of plant was prized all over Europe, as far fewer specimens had generally been brought back from earlier expeditions. The explorer left these and other exhibits, such as African utility items and objects d'art to the Royal Prussian Museum in Berlin. After his return in 1876, Pogge settled in the Hanseatic city of Rostock, where he worked on the publication of his diary notes.

> Paul Pogge
> Informations- und
> Begegnungsstätte
> 17166 Zierstorf
> Tel. +49(0)039976
> 541-0

In these writings, he did not just report on the flora, fauna and climate of the newly discovered country, but also on the fascinatingly alien cultures. In contrast to the later colonial rulers, Pogge and Homeyer shared a reverence for the customs and traditions of the original African inhabitants.

During his second expedition, starting in Luanda in present-day Angola, at the side of the African explorer Herrmann von Wissmann, Pogge and his companions planned to set up a station to grant new opportunities. While Wissmann took another route to the Indian Ocean, Pogge followed the original plan and monitored the station set up near present-day Kananga for over a year. This period of deprivation so wore away at Pogge's health that he undertook the arduous return march through swamps, pathless forests and rivers to Luanda. Here, the explorer succumbed to a lung complaint on 16th March 1884.

A monument in the Rosengarten in Rostock commemorates the Africa traveller Pogge.

Many newspapers reported the tragic death of the Africa traveller. Thereafter, however, his merits gradually sank into oblivion, although no other scientist up to that time had lived alone among African people as long as Pogge. The explorer was falsely branded a racist after 1945 and the bust erected in the Rostock Rose Garden was removed. Today, thanks to the initiative of dauntless citizens, Pogge is again enthroned in his old position. The Ethnological Museum in Berlin still guards some of the treasures brought back by Paul Pogge. There are still about 60 items in the collection, three of them with a regular place in the permanent exhibition "Art from Africa". There is also an exhibition in the old farm house at Ziersdorf near Teterow, Pogge's birthplace.

Record-breaking oak trees in Mecklenburg

Huge trees in Ivenack are among the oldest in Central Europe

The oldest specimen is estimated to have stood firm for 1,200 to 1,300 years. The six ancient giants rise up 35 metres into the sky in the middle of an expansive deer reserve in Ivenack near Demmin. With girths of around 11 metres, it takes 12 people to embrace each of the trees. The oaks indicate that the region around Ivenack was already densely populated in the Slav period. They are relics of a medieval form of land use, in which domestic animals were driven into woods known as "Hudewälder" (wood to herd livestock). Since the light-loving oaks were a valuable source of food for pigs, they were never cut down and thus had ideal conditions for their development.

The oaks have inspired human imagination for a long time.

According to a legend, seven nuns from the Cistercian convent at Ivenack broke their vows and were transformed into oak trees. After a thousand years, the first of the seven was redeemed, whereupon one of the oaks died. It is said that one nun will be redeemed every hundred years until all the oaks have fallen. For the sake of future generations, it is to be hoped that this is just a myth, so that Ivenack, with its wonders of natural history, can continue to attract guests from Germany and all over Europe.

The two sides of aerospace

Peenemünde 1942 – rocket weapon goes into space

In 1923, the physicist Hermann Oberth published an investigation into the technology of space travel under the title "Die Rakete zu den Planetenräumen" (The Rocket into Interplanetary Space), thereby provoking a wave of massive interest in rocket technology. Among those who swam on this wave was the director Fritz Lang, who brought out his film "Frau im Mond" (Woman in the Moon) in 1929. At this time, rocket researchers were still pursuing civilian questions, investigating for example the deployment of meteorological or mail-carrying rockets. It was only at the end of the 20s as liquid-propellant engines were gaining increasing attention that the military became interested because liquid-propelled rockets are independent of the surrounding medium and know no boundaries as far as height and speed are concerned. Liquid fuels are much more powerful and open up more favourable control options for a large missile. Thus, in 1929, the Army Weapons Office had the military applicability of liquid-fuel rockets tested and supported the Berlin-Tegel rocket launch site. Enthusiasts such as Rudolf Nebel, Hermann Oberth and Klaus Riedel worked there. The Society of Space Travel was also joined at the start of the 1930s by the physics student Wernher von Braun. Just two years later, in 1932, von Braun came to work for Walter Dornberger in

Internet tip:
www.peenemuende.de

Kummersdorf near Berlin, where the German Armed Forces had set up a Test Centre West for rockets. In the following years, Dornberger and von Braun formed a team of researchers, which in 1936 comprised more than 70 members. They experimented, tested and constructed, tested rocket forms, injection machines for the fuel etc. They tried to stabilise the rockets' flight and improve the control. Step by step, the rockets on the test stands got bigger and heavier.

In 1936, Dornberger and von Braun persuaded the German military of the military possibilities of the rockets. Millions in sponsorship were approved, if it were possible to "make a usable weapon out of rocket propulsion". Construction work on the most expensive "armourer's" of the "Third Reich" began at Peenemünde in the same year. The town on Usedom was ideal for the project. Its island location made it easier to keep secret and allowed undisturbed test firings along the coast.

The administration building was moved into in April 1937, facilities and accommodation followed. In spring 1938, over half the planned production facilities and test stands were assigned.

Development in the following years was principally shaped by General Dornberger, Head of Rocket Development, and von Braun as Technical Director. Hundreds of scientists and thousands of technicians worked beside them. As, with the start of war, not only material shortages were occurring, but also the shortage of workers became ever greater, forced foreign labour was increasingly used from 1940 next to mobilised German workers as were, from 1943, concentration camp prisoners.

> Historisch-Technisches Informationszentrum
> Im Kraftwerk
> 17449
> Peenemünde
> Tel. +49(0)38371 5050

On 3rd October 1942 the first rocket was successfully launched from the test bed in Peenemünde.

The first rockets were successfully launched at this time. On 3rd October 1942, in the thickly wooded grounds of the army test base, the fourth test prototype of the A 4 long-distance rocket was ready for firing at test stand 7. At 15.58 hours, the rocket rose over the forest. The launch command had been given by Commander Dornberger by microphone to the test stand engineers. The military followed events on the television screen – Peenemünde was equipped with cutting-edge technology. It was already the fifth launch attempt in eight months. A peak height of twelve kilometres had been reached as early as August. But the goals were more ambitious, as after the lost air battle against Great Britain, Dornberger had promised Adolf Hitler a "V-weapon" in the summer of 1941, which would have a range of 300 km, hit the Britons and be able to reduce London to rubble.

The 14t-heavy rocket took off effortlessly, reached a height of 84.5 km at supersonic speed and smashed into the Baltic Sea 192 kilometres away. Rejoicing was unconfined. The engineers had got a whole lot closer to the stars! The military celebrated a weapon of new dimension. They had a long-distance rocket against which there was as yet no defence. Unless the production facilities were destroyed.

On the basis of information from various sources, Allied bombers attacked Peenemünde in 1943, severely damaging the production plants. Serial production of the rocket, the so-called "wonder weapon V2", had to be moved to a Mittelwerk underground factory near Nordhausen in Harz. The concentration camp Mittelbau-Dora also came into being here. In inhuman conditions, prisoners rapidly constructed production facilities and started serial production of the terror weapon. Of the approximately 60,000 people from 21 countries who worked here between 1943 and 1945, about 20,000 did not survive this hell.

About 3,200 long-distance A4/V2 rockets were fired from September 1944 to March 1945, killing about 5,000 people – principally British civilians.

Internet tip:
www.tlm-mv.de

What remains? The formidable financial-and-human-resource-swallowing rocket was a failure from the military point of view, as it did not reverse the course of the war. After the war ended, the Nazi rocket technology accelerated the development of the space rocket, without which the satellites could not reach space. It also paved the way for intercontinental missiles. Fitted with atomic warheads, they played a central role in the Cold War. Engineers such as Wernher von Braun never questioned the inhuman Nazi system of slavery which enabled their rockets to be built. To date, no words of remorse have come to light.

The Brockhaus plot

Malchin inventor developed first petrol-powered vehicle

Who invented it? In the case of the car, the whole world knows the answer: Gottlieb Daimler and Carl Benz, of course! But that view of history ignores an important contributor to the development of today's number one form of transport. For the history of its invention was 'Aryanised' by the Nazis.

The racially motivated distortion of history began in 1940. Evidently in response to a request by Daimler-Benz AG, the notorious Reich Propaganda Ministry notified the concern on 4th July that it had issued an order to the publishers of encyclopaedias that the inventor of the modern motor-car was no longer to be cited as the (Jewish) engineer Siegfried Marcus from Malchin in Mecklenburg, "but the two German engineers Gottlieb Daimler and Carl Benz".

Siegfried Marcus achieved a milestone for the development of the automobile.

"That is why we learned at school that the sole inventors of the automobile were Daimler and Benz," says Prof. Dr. Peter Clemens. Shaking his head, he adds, "We could say it is a remnant of Nazi ideology that has continued up to the present day."

The medical practitioner and genealogy enthusiast from Schwerin knows what he is talking about, because he is related to Siegfried Marcus. And as such he is in no doubt: "Whilst it is true that Marcus was not the designer of the first car suitable for serial production, if you ask who constructed the first petrol-powered

The second of Marcus' vehicles can be seen in the Viennese Museum of Technology.

Internet tip: www.tmw.at

car, then the answer in my opinion is clear: Siegfried Marcus!"

The versatile inventor built his first, rather primitive car as early as 1864, says Clemens, who heads a paediatric hospital. "At some point between 1872 and 1875 he built the second one – and that was still ten years before Daimler and Benz", he adds.

Historians are somewhat more reserved in their judgement. The frequently cited story of the invention of the first petrol engine is probably a legend, says historian Dr Wolf Karge. "But what is beyond doubt is that the electric ignition and hence also the contact breaker were invented by Marcus," says Karge. "And so he laid a very important milestone in the development of the car."

In the Vienna Technical Museum (TMW), which has held the precious original of Marcus' second car since as early as 1915, the dispute over who was first is treated with nonchalance. It is proudly stated that, "This is clearly the oldest drivable automobile in the world". According to TMW spokesperson Barbara Hafok, there are documents proving beyond all doubt that the engine was produced around 1888 to 1889. "And as far as we are concerned that is the date of its invention," she argues, "for without an engine there can be no car."

They also say in Vienna: "What is relevant for us is that Siegfried Marcus was one of the most brilliant inventors in the world – and he was also Austrian."

But at that point we insist on adding that he originated from Mecklenburg!

The Grande Dame of Esperanto

Schwerin poet was the first to versify in the artificial language

It was a late fruition: at the age of 61, Marie Hankel goes back to school. Together with the grammar school teacher Gotthilf Sellin, the woman from Schwerin learns Esperanto – and discovers a fascinating new world beyond her cheerless widow's life since the early death of her husband 28 years before. The woman from a well situated permanent secretary's family plunges with enthusiasm into the dissemination of the still-fresh idea of Esperanto.

More than ever after moving to her daughter's home in Dresden. On the Elbe, Marie Hankel quickly distinguishes herself as a respected organiser of Esperanto congresses. In 1907/1908, she is instrumental in arranging the 2nd German Esperanto congress in Dresden and in 1908 also takes over the editorship of the cultural journal La Bela Mondo.

This painting of Marie Hankel was created by order of the Dresden Esperanto Centre.

In the same year, reports the Schwerin chronicler Ralf Kuse, she is the first woman of any description to be present on the congress committee of the 4th Esperanto world congress taking place in Dresden. The major event, organised under the patronage of the King of Saxony, is also attended by the globally venerated inventor of Esperanto Dr L. L. Zamenhof, with whom Marie Hankel takes up an intensive correspondence. Zamenhof's last unfinished letter before his death on 8th April 1917 is addressed to her.

It is no wonder that, from being a "simple" Esperantist, she came to be seen virtually as a kind of female "disciple" of the Majstro, "Master" L.L. Zamenhof, writes the Cologne linguist Bernard Pabst. "The day which established Marie Hankel's historical fame as the first Esperanto poet was 8th September 1909, when, as a 65-year-old, she was selected as the first "flower queen" at the 5th Esperanto world congress in Barcelona for her poem La simbolo de l' amo (The Symbol of Love)", adds the scientist. "From then on she was seen as the Grande Dame of the German Esperanto movement."

"The quality of her poems however should be seen in relation to their time", qualifies the Vienna Esperanto expert Herbert Mayer. "By modern criteria they sound rather naive."

Nevertheless, they struck a nerve for an up-and-coming, cosmopolitan language community. And as well as her services to the light Muse, Marie Hankel makes an extremely serious contribution to a modern image of women. With her commitment as a congress organiser and performances in her own right such as a speech at the 6th Esperanto world congress at Washington in 1910 on women's suffrage. "There was work here that I could do; here my activity was useful, indeed necessary. ... It was a delight to be alive!", writes the fervid Esperantist about her late-discovered calling.

This enthusiasm remained with her till her death: Marie Hankel died in Dresden at the age of 85. On 15th December 1929 – the birthday of the Majstro Zamenhof. The metropolis on the Elbe gave the Schwerin woman a memorial: since 2003, a street has borne the name of the founder of Esperanto literature.

Internet tips:
www.esperanto-gb.org
www.esperanto-usa.org

Neubukower bared advanced culture

Heinrich Schliemann brought to light 1,000 years of Greek history

In the blazing sun, the archaeologist is kneeling in front excavated finds. Exhausted and eager, but carefully he removes the dust of the last thousand years from the valuable artefacts. Doing so, he discovers objects of astounding artistic accomplishment.

Such or the like newspapers such as *The London Times* may have reported on Heinrich Schliemann's excavations in his day.

The Greeks claim with justification that a Mecklenburger gave them back 1,000 years of their history. The father of archaeology, Heinrich Schliemann (1822-1890), dug in Mycenae and thereby provided access, not only for the Greek people, to the first advanced culture in mainland Europe.

Born in the year 1822 in the small town of Neubukow near Bad Doberan, Heinrich Schliemann spent his early childhood in Ankershagen. According to legend, the inquiring youngster got a "World History for Children" as a present from his father and thereafter dreamt of excavating the legendary Troy.

The pastor's son came from humble circumstances, received a poor education, yet developed a remarkable ambition to become a successful man. The linguistically gifted Mecklenburger made his way to Amsterdam and to Russia; later he travelled the world as a well-to-do businessman. But changeful as his life was, he never lost sight of his great desire. From 1866 to 1868, Schliemann studied the Greek language and archaeology at the Sorbonne in Paris and settled in Athens in 1869. In the 17-year-old Greek woman Sophia Engastromenos he found not just a wife and mother of two of his children, but a true companion: she shared his passion for Homer and for archaeology. She supported him in his unusual enterprise and endured with him the stresses and strains that his work entailed.

Filled with determination, Schliemann betook himself to Hissarlik. He interpreted the old writings quite differently from his predecessors and was frequently treated with amusement. Spade in hand and Homer in head he sought unerringly in the present-day region of Turkey for the city of Troy – where the ancient Greeks of the Iliad had settled, and in 1873 actually found the incredible Treasure of Priam. Today we know that the treasure is to date back until about 2250 B.C. and thus is even thousand years older than Schliemann reckoned. This unbelievable discovery spurred him on to search in Greece as well.

In the Bronze Age city Mycenae, of which the Cyclopean walls and Lion Gate were already visible, he made an unusual discovery in 1876: the explorer excavated graves, finding bones and a wonderfully preserved mummy. With these graves, the archaeologist discovered what is surely one of the oldest monumental structures in the whole of Europe: the shaft graves of Mycenae. But he thereby endowed the world not merely with an archaic structure; the writings of Pausanias had lead Heinrich Schliemann to the traces of an entire culture of the 16th century B.C. Filigree burial objects sug-

> Heinrich-Schliemann-Museum
> Lindenallee 1
> 17219
> Ankershagen
> Tel. +49(0)39921 3252

gested a well-developed culture, indeed the first advanced culture in mainland Europe. They included a mask, which went down in history as the golden mask of Agamemnon.

The man from Mecklenburg became an international celebrity. His proud homeland also recognised his merits. The University of the Hanseatic City of Rostock in Mecklenburg awarded the scientist a doctorate *in absentia*. The honours and the extraordinary discovery in Mycenae later emboldened the scientist to search for prehistoric evidence in Tiryns and Orchomenos and on Crete as well. If Schliemann did not always interpret his finds correctly, he did bring to light the legendary Mycenaean culture (16th-12th century B.C.). Schliemann's approach to archaeology as a science of entire cultures is still ground breaking. In 1876, Schliemann donated his rich find to the National Archaeological Museum in Athens, where it can still be marvelled at today.

Original ceramic finds and replicas of many other treasures, such as the famous golden mask, can be admired by tourists and locals alike today in the only Schliemann museum in the world at Ankershagen. Visitors are welcomed to the site by an impressive Trojan horse. There is indisputably no better place to put oneself into position to understand the life and work of Schliemann than his home town of Ankershagen, where the ten-year-old once dreamt of Troy, the "World History for Children" on his lap.

Heinrich Schliemann is deemed to be the rediscoverer of Troy.

Internet tip:
www.mnsu.edu

Stralsund chemist discovered oxygen

Late honour for decent experimenter

The discoverer of Oxygen, Carl Wilhelm Scheele, is very often registered as Swedish chemist in Encyclopaedia. Few are familiar with the fact that the ambitious experimenter, who conducted 20,000 tests, originated from Stralsund in Western Pomerania. After the war, the Peace of Westphalia (1648) handed the town of Stralsund to Sweden.

Presumably, due to this supremacy the son of a merchant served his apprenticeship in Gothenburg in 1775. Employed as apothecary's assistant in Malmo, Stockholm and Uppsala, he acquired detailed knowledge of chemistry. At Uppsala University he socialised with well-known professors, among them Carl von Linné and Torbern Bergmann, the leading Swedish chemist. Scheele is said to soon have surpassed Bergmann in knowledge and skills. Nevertheless, he did not devote himself to science, but became proprietor of pharmacy at Köping. Two years later, he became member of the Royal Academy and graduated in pharmacy at the Collegium Medicum all at once.

Despite his business cares he was engaged in research. He worked hard at night and ambitiously journalised his examinations and it was worth it. He discovered "fire-air" experimenting with black oxide of manganese, oxide of mercury. The isolated gas was oxygen today, the meaning of which Scheele was not yet aware of. Unfortunately, the modest chemist

Internet tip:
www.koping.se/
kopingtemplates/
Page.aspx?id=1376

failed to publish his findings until after Joseph Priestley's announcement in 1774. The Englishman became known as discoverer of oxygen when he obtained it independently. Scheele, by contrast, did not publish his book "Chemical Treatise on Air and Fire" including investigations on oxygen, until 1777.

Moreover, he investigated uric acid, discovered chlorine and baryta, analysed lactic acid and hydrogen fluoride. In his pharmacy in Köping he analysed ammoniac, nitrogen and many other chemical elements such as manganese, barium and tungsten. He was the first to obtain tungstic acid from the mineral tungsten, since named scheelite. A pigment called Scheele's green carries his name since he prepared it from copper arsenites.

Karl Wilhelm Scheele gave oxygen the name "fire air".

Quite unaware of of many substances' poisonous character, Scheele also ascertained smell and taste of every substance he worked with, which was presumably one of the reasons for his early death in 1786.

Görnower saves palm trees

Bioacoustics specialist Benedikt von Laar exposes a hidden pest

"I actually find it very beautiful", says Benedikt von Laar as he examines the shiny rusty-red beetle in the transparent cylinder on his living room table. The insect with the remarkable projecting snout slowly changes position. Despite the warmth from the crackling stove in the manor house of Klein Görnow, a few more degrees would be needed in order for "rhynchophorus ferrugineus" to feel really comfortable. But the striking insect known in English as the red palm weevil is all the more active a few degrees of latitude further south of this village in the Warnow Valley close to Warin.

beetle costs Saudi Arabia 120 million dollars per year

"In Saudi Arabia alone, it causes damage to the tune of 120 million dollars a year", says the 41-year old head of the Bioacoustics and Consulting firm BvL on the basis of his experience of collaboration with Saudi governmental authorities since 2001. The strategy of the little gourmet is quite simple: "Go for anything that looks like a palm tree." The beetle excavates small cavities into the trunk just under the ground or makes tiny holes in the base of the leaves and then lays its eggs there, explains von Laar. In the protective environment of the palm trunk, a new generation of beetles can then grow up, happily munching away at the plant from the inside, without being noticed from the outside. "That continues until the palm breaks apart", says van Laar, a qualified biology and geography teacher, landscape ecologist and IT expert. "Then you suddenly have a problem with 300 to 600 beetles whose sole purpose in life is to find the next palm."

The native of Bottrop already has the biggest problem under control: by using a unique high-tech listening device, he can now identify affected plants at an early stage by detecting the extremely faint sounds made by the weevil grubs, rather than only being able to determine which plants are affected when the little nibblers have completed their work of destruction. "The detector works at an amplification of 80 decibels – that means we raise the sound level to that of a jet", explains the inventor, whose motto is "Where others give up, we get going." With this invention, the company from the tiny village of just 18 people in the Warnow Valley has caught the attention of specialists worldwide. In April the bioacoustics expert will be travelling to the Emirates to give talks at the invitation of UN bodies and the Saudi Ministry of Agriculture. The BvL devices developed with a flexible network of specialists from all over Germany are already in operation not only in Saudi Arabia but also around the city of Valencia in Spain, in the Italian region of Palermo, on Rhodes, Crete and the Canary Islands. "Beforehand, however, each country has had to learn the hard way", says the big man with the bushy beard who stands 2.03 metres tall. "First they try pesticides, which kill off everything around, including the beetle's competitors, but which do not reach the beetles themselves because they are protected within the trunk."

The "Rhynchophorus ferrugineus" damages palms extensively.

Internet tip:
www.laartech.biz

Then pheromone-baited traps are used which only achieve one thing: "They attract the beetles en masse."

Sometimes that does, however, at least set them in the right direction, says von Laar with a wry smile. In Spain, for example, eager civil servants had dotted the garden of the Spanish Environment Minister with such traps. "He was extremely annoyed when after a few weeks his favourite trees came crashing down, and that's when they contacted us."

> In some regions up to 90 per cent of the palms are infested with beetles.

"Using bioacoustics, I have a detection rate of 97 per cent", he says. Despite the highly sensitive equipment, however, it is a difficult process demanding a lot of experience and perseverance. Once the problem has been detected at an early stage, action must be taken quickly and determinedly. The direction in which the damage is spreading is established by means of satellite positioning – "so that you start at the front and does not end up chasing after the beetle", explains von Laar. Then the radical step must be taken: any affected trees have to be felled immediately and disposed of in a suitable way. "These trees are contaminated material", warns the expert. In practice, however, hair-raising mistakes are sometimes made: for example, when felled trees full of voracious nibbling insects are transported on open trucks.

According to nature-lover von Laar, the human factor is a core problem in general. He points out that it is man's "regulatory interference" in nature, with monocultures and chemical agents, that creates the conditions for invasions such as that of the red palm weevil.

This is made even worse by the demand for cheap products and the greedy pursuit of profits. In order to offer package tourists the "Ba-

Benedikt von Laar combats harmful insects using a "bugging operation".

hama feeling at a discount rate", huge numbers of palms have been imported from Egypt to the Canaries, Balearic islands etc., says von Laar. "And that was done despite the fact that up to 90 per cent of the palms in the Nile Delta are infested with beetles."

Via a seminar centre in Klein Görnow, the sustainability campaigner hopes to convey information about matters like these to people around the world as a way of helping them to help themselves. For example, von Laar demonstrated to a group of Tibetans the advantages of nature parks. And for good reason: in their country, the nouveaux riches are in the habit of driving speed boats across ecologically sensitive mountain lakes.

The acoustics expert from Klein Görnow is now gaining a reputation even further afield. And restorers from Vienna who look after the tombs of famous individuals buried in the city's Central Cemetery, such as Beethoven and Brahms, have appealed to him for help. "An extremely rare species of weevil has appeared there and is eating away at the coffins."

Wismar's Count von Count

Gottlob Frege invented the principles of programming languages

Professor Frege would surely have felt honoured. After all, the road named after him in Wismar leads directly onto the road called Philosophenweg. Gottlob Frege (1848-1925) is regarded as one of the most influential thinkers of the late 19th/early 20th century and as a pioneer of mathematical logic. But outside the German and international circle of experts, few people are aware of his contribution to informatics, among other things.

Frege developed formal logic, enriched linguistic philosophy with his ideas on the meaning of words and was the first to define the concept of number.

Frege, who studied and taught in Göttingen and Jena, is still honoured in Wismar. Uwe Lämmel, professor of informatics at the college of higher education there, learned about the famous scion of the town during his student years. "Frege was not properly understood by his contemporaries; it was not until later that his work was appreciated", explains Lämmel. Frege's contribution is so logical that it makes one wonder why no-one else thought of it before.

At the centre of his approach to logic is what is called 'implication' – better known in everyday life as the 'if-then principle'. 'If the book is good, I will recommend it.' Using Frege's concept, we can also say that the condition applies to all objects: i.e. 'in the case of all books, if the book is good, I will recommend it'. Frege also provides for the negation of these statements: 'the book is not good'.

"His description of these interconnections made the formal presentation of knowledge and the processing of knowledge by means of computers possible", says Uwe Lämmel. Frege's systematic presentation of conditions still forms the basis of programming languages.

The derivation of his definition of number is more complex. Frege starts from the principle that zero represents the quantity of all elements that are not identical with themselves.

Gottlob Frege thought in the If - Then categories essential today.

"Unfortunately, in Germany Frege is not given the recognition he deserves," says Professor Lämmel. Whereas a whole page is devoted to him in the "Encyclopaedia Britannica", he only merits a few lines in German encyclopaedias. But the people of Wismar are nevertheless proud of Gottlob Frege. There is not only a Frege Centre at the university that is dedicated to improving the teaching of mathematics. Every year the municipality of Wismar also awards the Frege Prize for the best final-year dissertations in the fields of Technology, Economics and Design. In May there is the traditional Frege Hike. "That is due to a special quirk of Frege's", says Uwe Lämmel, himself a member of the Frege Centre. "During his summer break he always hiked from Jena to Wismar."

In Jena the mathematician worked as an outside lecturer and later associate professor. After his retirement, Gottlob Frege spent his final years in Bad Kleinen on Lake Schwerin.

Chess Bible by Mecklenburg master

Paul Rudolf von Bilguer drafted leading reference book

Paul Rudolf von Bilguer is well known to chess players. He is the author of the standard work on the theory of the game. Bilguer was a member of the 'Plejaden' (Pleiades), a Berlin-based group of German chess masters in the 19th century. He was regarded as one of the most gifted of the masters. What is even more important for chess history are his studies in the field of the theory of chess. "Das Zweispringerspiel im Nachzuge" was a monograph published in 1839. He also worked on the planning and contents of a famous chess handbook, which was intended to present the theory of chess in a new way. Unfortunately, however, Bilguer died before he could complete it. He was only 25 years old. His friend and fellow chess player Tassilo von Heydebrand und der Lasa cited him as the author of the draft on the title page of the reference book that for nearly a hundred years came to be revered as the chess-player's bible all over the world. It was first published in 1843 and went into eight editions, each one being revised and expanded.

Bilguer was born in 1815 in Ludwigslust, Mecklenburg. His talent was recognised when he was still at the Pages' Institute in Schwerin, where he showed great interest in chess and literature. However, at his father's request, he did not devote himself to science or to chess after leaving school, but rather entered military ser-

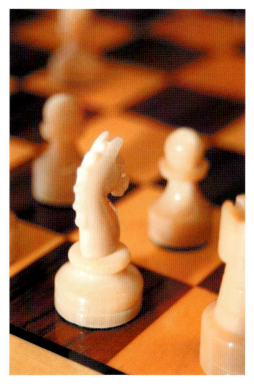

Chess – a game that fascinates people around the world.

vice. In 1837, he was transferred from Neuruppin, where he was initially stationed, to the Military Academy in Berlin, and there he came into contact with the "Berlin School", the said Pleiades. As a result of serious illness, he soon had to give up the idea of a career as a soldier and left the military. He then devoted himself entirely to his passion – and in this he was very successful: almost no other chess reference book has ever achieved such great importance as Bilguer's "Chess Bible".

Swedish royal visitors in Greifswald

Queen Silvia congratulates University on anniversary of its foundation

Queen Silvia visited the town on the Bodden on the 550th Anniversary of the Greifswald University.

Internet tip:
www.uni-greifswald.de

For over 150 years, the Ernst Moritz Arndt University of Greifswald was under the control of the Swedish crown. The main building was officially opened in 1750 by the Swedish king, Friedrich IV, himself. On the occasion of the 550th anniversary of the founding of the second oldest university in the Baltic region, the Queen of Sweden again appeared in person. After Her Highness Queen Silvia had arrived in Greifswald on the morning of 17th October, she reopened the restored Baroque assembly hall in the main building. Her arrival was greeted by more than 400 spectators.

The University of Greifswald owes its splendour to the period when most of West Pomerania was under Swedish rule. When it, along with the Island of Rügen, fell to Sweden after the Thirty Years War, the university – which had been founded in 1456 – benefited from the role of Greifswald as a regional administrative centre. Western Pomerania served Sweden as a supplier of grain and as a military outpost on the European mainland. The day-to-day business of government, however, largely continued to be conducted by native administrators. Today, the city's relationship with Sweden is very close and these ties are carefully cultivated. This is evident both in political and cultural relations and in the economic structure of Mecklenburg-Western Pomerania.

Dutchman engraved Pomeranian chronicle on copper plates

Early map was extraordinary detailed

The Lubin Map is the first comprehensive map of Pomerania. Philipp II, Duke of Pommern-Stettin in the 17th century commissioned what was for those days extraordinary map material. Philipp II aimed to compile a chronicle of Pomerania, decked out with illustrations and a map. He commissioned the Rostock University professor and theologian Lubinus, a painter from Antwerp, and an engraver from Amsterdam with the creation of the artwork, and these produced it with a love of detail. Consisting of 24 individual sheets, the map of Pomerania depicts genealogies and portraits, as well as 335 family crests of the Pomeranian dukes on the inside borders. Tablets contain geographical, historical and economic descriptions of the region. The border of the artwork is decorated with 49 images of towns, castles and monasteries.

Before he became Duke over Pommern-Stettin, Phillip II had studied in Rostock, travelled through many countries and moved in the society of scientists and artists. The Lubin Map was engraved on twelve copper plates each weighing six pounds, each 420 mm by 548 mm in size. Put together, the sheets produced an artwork measuring an incredible 1.25 by 2.21 metres. Unfortunately, Phillipp II did not live to see the extraordinary Pomerania map finished. He died a few months before its completion.

Internet tips:
ruegenwalde.com
pommersches-landesmuseum.de

The Lubin map is displayed on pages 206/207.

Royal landscape design in Western Pomerania

Swedish queen redesigned baroque park in Löbnitz

The Swedish Queen, Louisa Ulrika (1720-1782) initiated the redesigning of the Baroque estate and park complex of the town of Löbnitz, south of the Fischland-Darß-Zingst peninsula. The sister of the Prussian king, Friedrich II, better known as Frederick the Great, often stopped in Western Pomerania during her travels between Sweden and Berlin. During the period when her husband was in dispute with the Swedish imperial council over the role of the monarch, she even moved into the old manor house.

The Löbnitz Park dates back to Luisa Ulrika of Sweden.

She chose this grand residence because its builder, the army colonel Count Schwerin, had served as a soldier under the great Swedish king, Charles XII. In the 18th century, the park surrounding the house was redesigned at her bidding as a Baroque garden complex. The Queen evidently liked to visit the cool ivy and jasmine-covered grotto next to the stream near the house on hot summer's days. Behind it, the stream ran through the pleasure garden with its avenues of lime trees, its ornamental buildings and hedges. The old Löbnitz estate and park are still a lovely place to relax and dream.

Internet tips:
www.fischland-darss-zingst.de
www.amt-barth.de/loebnitz.htm

Searching for traces in Australia

Man from Rostock considered co-founder of the "Garden State" Victoria

The city of Melbourne honours a child of the city of Rostock to this day. He played a decisive roll in the development of the "Garden State" Victoria.

The twenty-two year-old pharmacist, and studied botanist, Ferdinand Jakob Heinrich von Müller was driven into the warmer Australian climate because of his health condition. Because of his enthusiasm for research and his interest in the world of exotic plants he was assigned the position of government botanist in 1853 in the colony of Victoria. He was also entrusted with the care of the Zoological Gardens in Melbourne from 1857. In his life time, he researched and traversed up to 43,000 km of what he described as "the most dangerous and godforsaken areas", in order to collect up to 2,000 varieties of plants, 800 of which were previously unknown.

To this day, one can still enter the world of Ferdinand von Müller through the wrought-iron gate of the Royal Botanical Gardens in Melbourne. The giant park consists of so many flowers that, at first glance, one cannot begin to discern its abundance of offerings. In front of the national herbarium, one can find the botanist himself, cast in bronze. Just as many treasures await visitors here. At every plant an interested visitor can imagine how the researcher, whether in the jungle or in the sparse

Heinrich von Müller left a green trace on the fifth continent and is honoured by a monument in Melbourne.

Australian outback, collected, identified and painstakingly carried them to his unique garden.

The impassioned botanist published 40 volumes in German, English and Latin. The diffusion of useful trees in Australia is owed to him. In addition, Müller discovered the method for distilling oil from eucalyptus leaves, from which medicine profits today. In order to recognize this success, the university in his home city awarded him, in absentia, a doctorate in medicine.

On the occasion of the 100th anniversary of the baron's death – this title had been bestowed upon him by the king of Wuerttemberg in 1871 – a honorary stamp was issued in Germany and Austria. Every two years, since 1904, the Australian Association for the Advancement of Science has awarded a Müller medallion for outstanding scientific service. Traces of him can also be found on the Australian map, with such places as Mount Mueller and Mueller Lake.

Internet tip:
www.rgb.vic.gov.au

Rostock beach-chair conquers the world

Striped beach furniture delights sun-worshippers on the Pacific coast

A 125-year old Rostock invention is now a feature on beaches in California and even in living rooms in Florida. Wilhelm Bartelmann invented Germany's number-one item of maritime furniture, the "Strandkorb" 125 years ago. Now the cosy striped beach-chair is even appreciated on the other side of the Atlantic. Bartelmann, a master basket-weaver from Rostock, was commissioned by Elfriede von Maltzahn to produce a "seat for the beach as protection against excessive sun and wind". Despite her rheumatic condition, she wanted to be able to enjoy the healthily bracing seaside climate. Bartelmann produced a single-seat chair made of cane and wickerwork in which Mrs Maltzahn immediately made herself comfortable on the beach in the Baltic Sea resort of Warnemünde.

Initially mocked by the envious as an "upright laundry basket", the snug appearance of the "beach chair" soon led to rapidly growing demand in Bartelmann's basket-weaving workshop. As early as 1883 a cosy model for two people was pro-

Elizabeth Bartelmann and her daughters also felt at home in the beach chair.

duced, and Wilhelm's wife Elisabeth Bartelmann established the world's first beach-chair rental business in Warnemünde near the lighthouse.

Since Bartelmann failed to patent his product and demand was constantly rising, beach chairs were soon being manufactured and developed further by other craftsmen. Thus new chairs with footrests, arm rests and site boards were designed and a model with an adjustable backrest. This was crafted by his former apprentice Johann Falk in 1897.

Bartelmann sold his chairs to many seaside resorts, from the North Sea to East Prussia. Having advanced to the position of Court Master Basket-Weaver, he then produced large quantities of beach furniture in his Rostock workshop, thus establishing the beach-chair industry. However, he regarded himself as a craftsman rather than a fabricant.

The beach chair has enjoyed growing popularity for the past 125 years. The cosy two-seat chairs are even appreciated on the other side of the Atlantic now. The company Paradise Sungarden, for example, is attracting customers all over Florida with the striped or check-patterned two-seaters, which now cut a good figure in inland gardens and beside swimming pools, and even in living rooms. Despite the growing worldwide demand, the chairs are still hand-woven, just as they were when first invented.

Internet tips:
www.bartelmann.com
www.paradise-sungarden.com

Shopping fun from Mecklenburg-Western Pomerania

Parent firm of KaDeWe located in Wismar

The famous KaDeWe is the largest department store in continental Europe – and few people realise that it has its origins in Mecklenburg-Western Pomerania. Businessman Rudolph Karstadt opened his first "Tuch-, Manufaktur- und Confectionsgeschäft" (Fabric, Textiles and Clothes Shop) with 1,000 Talers as starting capital in Wismar on 14th May 1881 on the basis of what was at the time a revolutionary business strategy: low but fixed prices and cash payment. Today, 125 years after its foundation, Karstadt Warenhaus GmbH is one of Germany's leading department store chains. With an annual turnover of 4.9 billion Euro (2006) and 32,000 employees, Karstadt now operates 90 large department stores and 32 specialist sports stores.

In 2006 the Karstadt department store in Wismar celebrated its 125th birthday.

The original Karstadt store, a historic building in the heart of Wismar's old town, which is a Unesco World Heritage Site, now has four sales floors. In the store's own museum, visitors can explore the history of the company in an office and strongroom preserved in their original form and fitted out with exhibits dating back to the late 19th century. The Kaufhof department store originated in the Hanseatic town of Stralsund a few years earlier. At the age of thirty, Leonhard Tietz opened a "Garn-, Knopf-, Posamentier- und Woll-Waren-Geschäft" (Yarn, Button, Haberdashery and Woollens Shop) on 14th August 1879 at Ossenreyer Strasse 31 in Stralsund, thus laying the foundations of the first German department store with little other than the conviction that excellent quality should be sold at fixed prices and against cash payment.

At that time, haggling and buying on tick were commonplace, but the new sales practices made goods cheaper and so soon became increasingly popular among customers. Tietz was also one of the first businessmen to grant his customers the right to exchange goods. What began in 1879 in an area of 25 square metres square developed over the following years and decades into a rapidly expanding company with a constantly growing network of branches. A year after its establishment, the "Tietz Family" had just ten employees; by 1914 – shortly before the death of the company's founder – the statistics registered the total workforce as counting 6,200. When the National socialist party was about to close the company down, it was renamed Kaufhof AG. The Jewish Tietz family escaped abroad.

Today, Kaufhof Warenhaus AG operates 133 branches in more than 80 German cities as well as 15 branches in 12 Belgian cities, and the "Kaufhof Family" consists of around 27,000 employees.

Internet tip:
www.karstadt-unternehmen.de

Ohio sings ode to Baltic Sea island

Rügen song of home rediscovered in the USA

"Wenn die Granitz wieder grün wird..." the choir of the German Club in Columbus/Ohio belts out its ode to the Isle of Rügen in the choicest German. It is not just the language which is special, though. The song had already sunk into oblivion on Rügen itself. It had not been heard on the Baltic Sea island since the 1940s. "Whereas we had often sung it at school", remembers Herbert Jahn from Trent. Many of Jahn's schoolfellows had left the island after the Second World War. Adalbert Garbe for example ended up in the Rhineland, his brother Günter even emigrated to the USA. Here, long after their schooldays, the Rügeners heard their song again, and started searching in Germany for the text and sheets of music.

The schoolfellows saw each other again in 1994 in Wiek, on the island of their birth, at a reunion of the Golden Confirmands. Adalbert Garbe told a fellow pupil, who was apparently in contact with the daughter of the teacher, of his unsuccessful search for the Rügen song. Shortly afterwards, the latter contacted the searcher, for she had tracked down the song, by an unknown composer, between the old sheets of music from her time in the Wiek choir.

The eventful story of the "Ode to the Granitz" prompted another person born on Rügen, Eckhard Bode, to rescore the song.

A CD with the new recording of "Ode an die Granitz" can be obtained from the Tourism Association of Mecklenburg-Western Pomerania by calling the number +49(0)381 4030610 or via email to presse@auf-nach-mv.de.

Counterpart to Chicago's Reuter statue

Honour of the poet following American model

In Chicago, the Mecklenburg writer Fritz Reuter is honoured even more than in Rostock, his place of work? The Shanty-Choir "De Klaashahns" could not accept that. "De Klaashahns" are Rostock's musical calling card. Since 1964, the northerners in sailors' togs have been persuading listeners at home and abroad with their songs of the culture of the Baltic Sea coast. On their Chicago trip, the singers actually wanted to acquaint the Americans with their Mecklenburg roots, but also profited with a brilliant idea.

To their amazement, the Mecklenburgers came across a monument to their regional poet, Fritz Reuter (1810-1874), in Chicago's Humboldt Park. Here he stands, incidentally not far away from his better-known fellow German poets Goethe and Schiller. He was placed here in the 19th century on the initiative of Mecklenburg emigrants remembering their homeland, who evidently scrimped and saved to pay for the statue.

Reuter had immortalised the city of Rostock, home of the Klaashahns, in his works. He had praised the port town as the new Athens, Warnemünde as its Piraeus. This led the Klaashahn crew to ponder the fact that the much praised Hanseatic city indeed honoured the poet with street and district names, but not with a monument. Choir member Peter Struck in particular went about an unusual project. He set up the Fritz-Reuter-Plastik working party and collected votes and money for the erection of a statue in Rostock, similar to the exemplar in Chicago.

The working group called an artistic competition, in which 13 local sculptors took part. A jury deemed a somewhat larger-than-life statue by the artist Thomas Jastram the best. The sculptor, from a well-known artistic Rostock family, modelled and built, and his model was transformed into Bronze. After two years of hard teamwork and with the aid of generous sponsors, the Reuter effigy was hoisted onto its pedestal, on the occasion of the 130th anniversary of his death, in the Rostock Reutershagen district and ceremonially unveiled on 9th July 2004.

The bronze Fritz Reuter directs his gaze at Alt-Reutershagen, a quarter where many of his literary figures are still present in the form of street names. The poet played a major role in the revival of the Low German language in the 19th century. His works also won recognition in other languages and cultures though; some of them were even translated into Japanese.

Thomas Jastram created this statue of Fritz Reuter for Rostock.

The revolutionary coupling

Wismar invention initiates the great age of the railways

"A prophet is not without honour save in his own country." This biblical saying is also applicable to the railway pioneer from Wismar, Karl Scharfenberg (1874-1938). The coupling he invented over 100 years ago is just as important now as it was then. Without it, the development of high-tech fast trains like France's TGV and Germany's ICE would not have been possible. Many modern rail vehicles, from the express trains and locomotives of the Deutsche Bahn and its private competitors to the low-floor articulated light rail car, are equipped with Scharfenberg's centre puffer coupling (known in German as the "Scharfenberg-Mittelpufferkupplung").

The Mecklenburg inventor registered his patent on 18th March 1904. But even after its 100th anniversary, there is almost nothing anywhere in Germany to commemorate this great scion of Wismar. But now a college of higher education, Hochschule Braunschweig/Wolfenbüttel, has named its Faculty of Transport, Sport and Tourism, located in Salzgitter, after Karl Scharfenberg.

After all, his invention had major consequences not only for technical development but also for safety. The formerly customary fitting of rail vehicles with buffers and hook couplings to connect the wagons had given rise to one of the most dangerous railway jobs, that of the coupler. In order to connect or disconnect wagons and locomotives, the coupler had to pass between or under the buffers and fasten or release the central screw coupling.

This had led to frequent accidents – particularly in America. There, the President had personally intervened and demanded in sharp tones the introduction of a centre puffer coupling as a statutory requirement. Scharfenberg's innovation was that with his system the vehicles became connected simply by bumping gently into one another. The work that had previously been necessary to couple the vehicles, and more importantly the associated dangers, were thereby completely eliminated. In contrast to other designs, the couplings were fastened securely together, which gave them a certain degree

Without Karl Scharfenberg's coupling equipment high-speed trains like the ICE would be difficult to imagine.

Express train of the German Railways (Deutsche Bahn) equipped with the Scharfenberg coupling en route to Warnemünde

Internet tip: www.fh-wolfen buettel.de

of stiffness and reduced the danger of the vehicles breaking away in the case of collisions. Scharfenberg was born on 3rd March 1874 in Wismar. The Scharfenbergs were teachers, vergers and railwaymen. After primary and secondary school, Scharfenberg attended the Technikum (technical college) in Neustadt/Mecklenburg (now called Neustadt-Glewe), where he studied engineering. From 1896 onwards, he worked as an engineer in the "Eisenbahn-Waggon-Fabrik Eisengießerei und Maschinen- Bau- Anstalt L. Steinfurt" (a railway carriage factory, iron foundry and machine-building company) in Königsberg in East Prussia (now Kaliningrad, Russia). It was there, in 1904, that he developed the centre buffer coupling for railway carriages. It was regarded as the best automatic coupling device of the time. The first railway in Germany to be fitted with the "Schaku" was the independent narrow-gauge railway Memel-Pöszeiten-Licken, which adopted the coupling in 1909. It proved to be very successful.

It was next employed when the suburban railway network of Berlin was electrified. In 1928, the Berlin and Hamburg undergrounds followed suit, and from the mid-1930s the coupling was also used in the Argentine capital, Buenos Aires.

It can be said with complete justification that without the Scharfenberg coupling the great age of the railways in the mid-1930s would probably not have taken place. The extremely streamlined form of the carriages and the speed records on routes such as the Berlin-Hamburg line, which aroused such enthusiasm during that decade, would not have been possible without the Schaku.

Orange prince from Mecklenburg-Schwerin

Baltic nobility connected to Dutch dynasty

Queen Beatrix' grandpa played in the garden of Schwerin Castle. About one hundred years ago, on 7th February 1901, he married as Duke Heinrich of Mecklenburg-Schwerin the twenty-year-old Wilhelmina of Orange Nassau and followed his wife to the Netherlands. From this marriage came, on 30th April 1909, the later Queen of the Netherlands, Juliana of Orange-Nassau. She is the mother of the present Queen of the Netherlands, Beatrix Wilhelmine Armgard of Orange Nassau. These dynastic connections make Schwerin Castle a grand highlight on the "Oranier Route". The traces left behind by the European royal house of Orange Nassau in Mecklenburg-Western Pomerania among other places are to be discovered on this route. Schwerin forms one of the easternmost stations on the

Ancestors of Queen Beatrix belonged to the ruling family of Mecklenburg Schwerin.

tracks of the House of Orange. The "Niederländischer Hof" Hotel and the Dutch paintings in the gallery of the State Museum in Schwerin recall this past. The "Niederländischer Hof" was named that on the occasion of the marriage of Heinrich and Wilhelmina.

The museum's collection was mainly compiled by Duke Christian Ludwig II of Mecklenburg in the 18th century.

The Dutch royal house of Orange-Nassau goes far back to the 16th century. William of Orange (1533-1584), who continues to mould the collective consciousness of the Netherlanders into the present day, stands at the beginning of the legendary dynasty. The name of the royal house came into being through his legacy: the southern French principality of "Orange" and the connections to the Hessian castle "Nassau".

Internet tip:
www.koninklijkhuis.nl

Bad Doberan attracts VIPs

Europe's oldest racecourse located in Mecklenburg

A shrill bell rings out. The stalls spring open. The thoroughbreds dash off. The ground of the oldest racecourse on the European mainland still vibrates several times a year today under the hoofs of the racehorses. Between Bad Doberan and Heiligendamm High Society convenes.

When the seaside resort "Am Heiligen Damm" was founded under Duke Friedrich Franz I in 1793, the place became established as a centre of attraction for fine society. Counts and dukes organised horse races on the open fields and thus laid the foundation for the Bad Doberan racecourse. In the summer of 1822, the year of the founding of the Doberan Racing Club by the Grand Duke of Mecklenburg-Schwerin, classic thoroughbreds raced for the first time in Europe. One year later, the Grand Duke of Mecklenburg-Schwerin founded the Baltic Sea Racecourse and simultaneously laid down a body of rules and regulations on horseracing after the English model. Among the first participants were von Maltzahn, von Plessen-Ivenack and Wilhelm von Biel, who arrived with English mares. Hereditary Grand Duchess Alexandrine presented von Biel, as the first victor, with a silver ornamental cup. Today, one still enjoys here the colourful society of businesspeople, elegantly dressed women, racing fans, and tourists.

At the "Baltic Meeting 2007" the public along the race track joined in the excitement.

Internet tips:
www.ost-seerennbahn.de
www.bad-doberan.de

Pioneer of electricity and mentor of the Tsar

Rostocker won favour with Katharina II

The scientist was one of the inaugurators of electricity as we know it today. Franz Ulrich Theodosius Aepinus discovered pyroelectricity in the mineral tourmaline. He found out that electric polarisation took place in the crystal in reaction to changes in temperature and concluded that electricity and magnetism must originate from the same source, namely the creation of a force field. Aepinus experimented with the capacitor and with a device for conducting electrophoresis, i.e. for separating positively and negatively charged particles. Born in Rostock in 1724, he studied mathematics, first in his home-town and later in Jena. Working as an outside lecturer, he made a name for himself at Rostock University from 1747 onwards and was soon elected to the Berlin Academy of Sciences as a professor of astronomy. The St. Petersburg Academy also took an interest in the gifted scientist. There he won such great acclaim that Tsarina Katherina II entrusted him with the training and education of the heir to the throne, Grand-Duke Paul Petrovich.

Besides, his investigative work on lunar surface structures and his "Description of the World" published in 1759 brought him great renown at the court of Katherina II. He enjoyed this acclaim until he retired in 1798 at the age of 74. Aepinus died in what is now Tartu in Estonia in 1802.

> Aepinus reported on his discoveries in his book "An Attempt at a Theory of Electricity and Magnetism" in 1758.

Western-Pomeranian know-how on the Mekong

Ship builder from Anklam crafts pontoon boats in Cambodia

Laboratories, weekend houses, restaurants – all on the water, on the pontoon boat of a ship builder from Pomerania. Norbert Freude originates from Anklam and lives directly on the Mekong today. The 54 year-old crafts his floating constructions out of fibreglass in his small shipyard in the Cambodian capital of Phnom Penh.

Freude learned how to build boats in a small family business, the "The Boat Yard Freude

Norbert Freude converses with Buddhist monks on the banks of the Mekong.

Anklam". Initially he went to Vietnam in 1995 to construct naval and freight ships. Later he decided to establish a small shipping yard in Cambodia. In the meantime, the ship builder has been commissioned to do jobs for the UN and even for the royal house.

Asia has also brought Freude success in his private life. His partner Sofia is in word and in deed always by his side.

Rügen's chalk cliffs in Switzerland

Western Pomerania inspired Caspar David Friedrich to produce his masterpieces

They can be admired in St. Petersburg or Paris, in Winterthur or Vienna, the silhouettes of the Hanseatic towns, the redbrick churches and the Baltic coast – the most important painter of German romanticism, Caspar David Friedrich (1774-1840), brought Western Pomerania's landscapes to the world. One of the Greifswald man's best-known works, the famous "Chalk Cliffs on Rügen" is on display in Winterthur in Switzerland.

Around 1810, at the age of about 35, Friedrich stood at a peak of his fame. He exhibited at the academies in Berlin and Dresden – finding recognition and buyers. People visited him in his studio, extolled the feeling and nature in the pictures and his masterly painterly skills. Not only his artist colleagues paid him tribute, later Russian Tsar Nicholas I was an extraordinary lover of Friedrich's paintings. He paid a highly personal visit to the artist at his studio in 1820. He made him famous in Russian artistic circles and even when public taste was moving away from Friedrich again, the heir to the throne bought the Romantic's landscape paintings. The multitude of Friedrich's works still to be seen in St Petersburg's Hermitage today is largely due to his collector's fervour.

With his unmistakable style of painting, Friedrich also clearly had an influence on the Düsseldorf Academy of Art, whose reputation

The magnificent painting "Chalk cliffs on Rügen" today hangs in Winterthur.

grew abroad during and after the Late Romantic period in the mid 19th century. Many of the Academy's students went to the USA and took romantic stimuli to America with them.

After his death in 1840, Friedrich initially fell into oblivion, but his work has experienced an extraordinary renaissance since the start of the 20th century. Even directors such as John Ford are supposed to have been influenced by the Romantic movements and Friedrich's works in their selection of scenery for western productions. His work has been experiencing ever more attention, abroad as well. Exhibitions at the Tate Gallery in London in 1972, at the Metropolitan Museum in New York in 1991 and 2002 or in the Prado Museum in Madrid 1992 demonstrate Friedrich's international recognition.

After his first student days in Greifswald, Friedrich studied at the Copenhagen Academy of Art and moved to Dresden in 1798, ever and again holidaying in Western Pomerania. His honeymoon with Caroline in 1818 too led to Greifswald, Wolgast, Stralsund and onto the Isle of Rügen. It inspired him to paint the masterpiece "Chalk Cliffs on Rügen".

Internet tip:
www.hamburger-kunsthalle.de

Between Adriatic and Mare Balticum

Milanese painter captured Baltic Sea coast

Boats seesawing on a thunderous sea. Fishermen waiting fearful on the shore. A giant St. Christopher saves a child from the implacable waves. Gabriele Mucchi (1899-2002), the Milan centenarian painter, eternalised his impressions of "People in the Storm" on the wall of the small fishermen's church in Vitt at the northernmost point of the Isle of Rügen. From the 1930s onwards, Mucchi felt himself conjoined with the people and weathers of the Pomeranian Baltic Sea coast. The support, help and community spirit of fishermen and people in the storm are the main themes in his works. He was preoccupied with the fates of coastal dwellers and their powerlessness against nature.

The idea for a picture grew in Mucchi in 1979 during a visit to the little church with its great ogive windows, seventeen years after his guest professorship in painting at the Ernst-Moritz-Arndt University in Greifswald. The Italian did

Gabriele Mucchi designed a church wall in Vitt on Rügen.

not actually execute his idea however until 1990; in acrylics on four by six metres of church wall.

As a "wanderer between the worlds" (Mucchi), he commuted between Milan, Berlin and Greifswald. For him the Baltic Sea coast was the more austere antipole to the Adriatic coastal scenery of his Italian homeland.

Gabriele Mucchi may be considered one of the major Italian painters of the 20th century. His life spanned the entire 20th century and allowed Mucchi to witness almost the entire development of political history and of modern art.

Further reading:
H. Ewe / U. Böttcher, The Isle of Rügen, Rostock 2001

Outstanding representatives of artistic movements such as Futurism, metaphysical painting or New Objectivity were among his friends and acquaintances. In the Berlin of the 1920s and 30s, were Mucchi owned a studio for a time, he encountered – personally or in their then highly topical pictures – George Grosz, Otto Dix, Max Beckmann, Käthe Kollwitz and Karl Hofer.

The search for a realistic form or artistic expression linked him with Bertolt Brecht, whose "Life of Galileo" was illustrated by Mucchi in 1957. "Realistic painting," demanded Mucchi, "portrays the reality of things and events, but in such a way that this portrayal passes judgement on the human being – as an ethical, social category." After Mucchi had already founded the "Nuovo Realismo" in Italy together with Renato Guttuso and other artists, he placed his artistic endeavour inter alia at the University of Greifswald in the service of the young GDR, whose dogmatic inflexibility in the field of art he hoped to be able to break down.

Internet tip:
www.vinetamuseum.de

Mecklenburg scientist plumbs the depths

The sinking of the Titanic motivated the invention of sonar

The Titanic disaster that shook the world in 1912 awakened the ambitions of the Mecklenburg scientist Alexander Behm. Today his invention is part of the standard equipment on ships: the echo-sounder.

At the time of the disaster Behm was head of a physics and technology research institute in Vienna. The inventor immediately began working on a device that would be able to prevent such tragedies in future. His idea was that the icebergs would reflect the sound waves, thus enabling ships' crews to detect them even under water with adequate time to prevent a collision. His invention was revolutionary, because the sea-floor and other ships did reflect the sound waves, just as Behm had hoped. Thus, the device prevented ships from colliding and running aground.

Passionate anglers may well have heard of the Behm Fly, which was another brain-child of the inventor of the echo sounder.

Alexander Behm was born in the small Mecklenburg town of Sternberg in 1880 and, contrary to what one might expect, he was not a good school student. Behm was brilliant, however, when it came to practical work. The patent on Behm's sonar device was so successful that in 1921 he was able to establish his own factory, the "Behm-Echolot-Fabrik". He also applied for 100 further patents. Many of them won him great acclaim both in Germany and abroad. For example, the Netherlands and France awarded him.

Master of the pipes

Wilhelm Sauer from Mecklenburg
built 1,100 organs

The pipes of the imposing organ in the Tallinn Cathedral regularly blast forth concerts through this house of God. Although located in Estonia, this work of art, upon which every Saturday an organist muses, originates from the hand of a virtuoso Mecklenburger from Schönbeck, near Friedland in Mecklenburg.

Located more than 1,000 kilometres from the Tallinn Cathedral is the workshop of organ builder Wilhelm Sauer. It was in this workshop that he successfully completed Tallinn's masterpiece between 1913 and 1914. Work on the organ had begun 35 years prior to its completion by his colleague Friedrich Ladegast. Sauer learned his craft in his father's workshop in Friedland near Neubrandenburg, and also during several study trips. His mentor was self-taught, but had built such an impressive instrument for the church near Schönbeck in 1835 that the Grand Duke of Mecklenburg-Strelitz gave him a scholarship to be educated as an organ builder.

Internet tip:
www.sauerorgelbau.de

In 1848 the son followed in his father's footsteps. Later study trips to Paris, Ludwigsburg, England and Switzerland brought him the necessary experience and he was soon put in charge of a subsidiary in Wałcz and he opened his on shop in Frankfurt/Oder in 1856. 1864 Wilhelm sent the first major organ to Berlin. Soon thereafter the churchgoers in Saint Petersburg were also listening to the delightful pipes from the Frankfurter Organ Firm. They were followed by 41 instruments from the Sauer workshop, all of which were sent to Russia. By the end of the 1860's, Sauer was receiving so many orders to construct organs that his firm could not keep up with the demand, although the firm had already been enlarged.

In addition to constructing organs, Sauer also dedicated himself to the improvement of the instruments. For his innovation of the "Combination gadget at organ stop knobs", he received the patent from the Imperial Patent Office in 1878. Sauer was decorated with several honours. 1883 he received the recognition as an "Academic Artist" from the Berlin Academy, the following year he was named the "Royal Court Master Builder". Between the years of 1857 and 1910 the artist created 1,110 of the most imposing instruments. As in the past, many organs from the Sauer workshop, like the one in the Tallinn Cathedral, continue to inspire enthusiasts and laymen in all parts of Germany, in several countries in Europe and even in South America and Asia.

Wilhelm Sauer followed in his father's footsteps with his organ building trade.

Baltic waves in the Dolomites

Declaration of love to the homeland girdles the earth

The "Baltic Sea waves" in the poem by Martha Müller-Grählert, a Low German regional poet, spilled over into the whole of Europe. She wrote it under the name "Mine Heimat" (My Homeland) as an ode to the Baltic Sea coast, which was set to music in Switzerland. Over the years and in many variations, the piece has come to be heard as the country song of many other regions in the world.

It is not that surprising that the people of East Frisia, Helgoland or East Prussia created their own modified versions, singing about the North rather than the Baltic Sea waves, the regions are after all not that far apart. It is all the stranger then that the song has penetrated so far inland that it still reverberates through the Dolomites today. The South Tyrolers sing about the flower-strewn meadows and tranquil mountains of their homeland in the Ladinic language. The hotelier Franco Dezulian from South Tyrol is supposed to have heard the song on the German coast after the Second World War and to have composed a version for the Fassa Valley in his Italian homeland in the night train going back. Today it is part of the repertoire of the local choral societies and Bozen Radio in Tyrol starts its local programmes with the tune.

Like the Pomeranians, the Swedes sing about the Baltic Sea waves, the Dutch about those of the North Sea. There are further versions in

Internet tip:
www.ostsee.de

> **Mine Heimat**
>
> Wo de Ostseewellen / Trecken an den Strand,
> Wo de gele Ginster / Bleuht in 'n Dünensand,
> Wo de Möwen schriegen, / Grell in't Stormgebrus –
> Da is mine Heimat, / Da bün ick tau Hus.

England and Spain. France sings about "Les Flots du Nord". It was probably brought to Canada, Australia and Brazil by emigrants. It is apparently even known in parts of Africa. Even though the song may have become a kind of worldwide success, Martha Müller-Grählert wrote it just for her homeland, the Baltic Sea coast. Born in Barth on the Fischland-Darß-Zingst peninsula, she worked in Berlin as a journalist from 1898 to 1911. Plagued by homesickness, she wrote the poem there. In 1907, it appeared in the "Meggendorfer Blätter", a music and art journal. The publication was read by a Thuringian living in Zurich, Simon Krannig, just as tormented by homesickness as Müller-Grählert. He was the conductor of the Zurich Workers' and Male Choral Society and wrote the tune to go with her verses and which went around the world.

In 1911, Martha Müller-Grählert went to Japan with her husband Dr. Max Müller, who was responding to a call to the University of Sapporo. After their return in 1915, the childless marriage broke up and Müller-Grählert got into economic distress. An acrimonious struggle broke out for the intellectual property rights to "Mine Heimat", which she and Krannig were ultimately awarded in 1936. This did not however alleviate her distress. Before the rights could bear material fruit, she died in Franzburg near her hometown Barth.

Marta Müller Grählerts waxed lyrical in her poem about Baltic waves, gorse on the dunes and screeching seagulls in the storm.

Executioner at Spyker Castle

Carl Gustav Wrangel beheaded on Rügen?

It is over 300 years since Carl Gustav Wrangel died in mysterious circumstances at Schloss Spyker on the island of Rügen. Even today, there are still legends and stories surrounding the Governor General of Swedish Pomerania. One legend has it that he was beheaded one night in 1676.

During the period of Swedish occupation, Queen Christina of Sweden gave the Count the old chateau known as Schloss Spyker on Rügen, and he had it altered in accordance with his tastes. In 1661 he ordered several tonnes of red chalk from Stockholm, with which he intended to give his property a striking outward appearance. He also had four fairy-tale towers added and had the ceilings in the first-floor rooms decorated with expensive stucco orna-

Carl Gustav Wrangel had Schloss Spyker given its typical colour.

mentation, which is regarded throughout the Baltic Region as an outstanding example of this type of decoration.

However, the palace was to prove his undoing. He died there in a mysterious way, giving rise to a gruesome legend which spread among the people of Rügen:

According to this story, the executioner was fetched from Stralsund on the evening before Wrangel's death. He was brought into a magnificent hall, where he was greeted by servants dressed in black. Wrangel was then carried ceremoniously into the hall on a black blanket, with his face covered and wearing his nightgown. The executioner then discharged his duties before being duly paid for his services and taken back to Stralsund.

It is more likely, however, that Wrangel passed away at Schloss Spyker in an unspectacular and non-violent way as a result of old age, sickness or exhaustion following his eventful military career.

Nevertheless, his ghost may well still haunt the house he so carefully restored, which today is a popular hotel. Apparently, a cold shiver still runs down the spines of guests when they hear the spooky story in the fitting atmosphere of the old restaurant in the chateau, which is called "Zum alten Wrangel".

Further reading:
H. Ewe / U. Böttcher,
The Isle of Rügen,
Rostock 2001

On the trail of the Tsars

Young daughter of the Tsar earns sympathy of Mecklenburgers

Internet tip:
www.schloss-ludwigslust.de

The Russian Tsar gave his approval for his then 14-year-old daughter Helene Paulovna's (1784-1803) engagement to the 22-year-old duke Friedrich Ludwig in 1799. Later in that same year all of St. Petersburg celebrated, both the engagement and the departure of the Tsar's daughter. With a convoy of approximately 30 coaches, the Tsar's daughter journeyed with her husband to Ludwigslust, where she then moved into the residence of Schwerin's dukes. An affectionate reception was prepared in Mecklenburg for the young Helene. 30 mounted farmers greeted the pair in Wöbbelin and accompanied their column all the way to the castle. Numerous receptions and celebrations took place in the following days thereafter. Helene quickly began to feel at ease in her new home, and her meekness and charitableness caused her to be much revered by Mecklenburg's citizens. In September of 1800, Helene gave birth to their first child, Paul Friedrich. Daughter Marie Luise was born three years later.

What had begun so magically, unfortunately, ended in tragedy. The princess contracted consumption and died in September of 1803. She was never able to reach the age of 19. She was entombed in the castle church, but was later transferred to a mausoleum. The mausoleum, that has been in the Ludwigslust castle park for 200 years, has recently undergone renovation and is a large attraction for tourists.

Expedition in the Lake Plateau

Henry M. Doughty travelled through "Old Merry Mecklenburg"

Columbus, Cook, and Darwin; Goethe, Arndt and Humboldt – all of them travelled around the world, in order to expand their horizons. It was not just the exotic lands which were of interest to scholars and inquisitive minds. English scholars managed to make it to Mecklenburg in the 18th and 19th centuries, which was home to Charlotte, their queen.

Henry Montagu Doughty set out on an unusual trip in 1890. It was not by train, by coach or by foot that he explored the unknown terrain of Mecklenburg with two of his daughters, butler, and seamen, but rather aboard the comfortable cargo ship Gipsy. The former royal naval cadet was looking for an adventure and

Doughty also sailed his ship on the Plau Lake.

found it in the Mecklenburg Lake Plateau. The team floated along to the "many towered Camelot", the castle in the Schwerin See, and then encountered the Rostock seven and gave an account of the "strange Astronomical Clock behind the high altar" in Rostock's Church Marienkirche. They marvelled at the Treptower Gate in Neubrandenburg, and sailed over the Müritz to Plau. In Mirow the adventurers strolled along looking for traces of the British queen Charlotte. The press in Mecklenburg followed the British visitors' expedition with great interest.

Doughty believed that he was the first to have explored Mecklenburg. However, Englishman Thomas Nugent had travelled the area already 100 years beforehand, in the year 1766, and had reported favourably on its land and people in his letters entitled "Travels through Germany, and primarily through Mecklenburg". The English journalist Charles James Apperley also discovered the Baltic Sea region some 60 years later.

Doughty, H. M. Our Wherry in Wendish Lands, from Friesland, through the Mecklenburg Lakes, to Bohemia. Botley 1985.

The adventure's travelogues, which arguably acted as a mirror for many in Mecklenburg, were translated into German sometime afterwards. Since 2001, Henry M. Doughty's adventure can still be read about in the German language. A good 100 years after Doughty's "discovery of Mecklenburg", "Mit Butler und Bootsmann" appeared, published by Quick Maritim Medien Rechlin.

Japanese loves to live by the Baltic Sea

Satoko Kojima brings Far East atmosphere to her adopted country

Satoko's fingers fly over the keyboard. Characters appear on the screen of her laptop which for most Germans just appear graceful. Satoko understands them all. She is translating the articles on the website of the Mecklenburg-Western Pomerania tourist board into Japanese.

Satoko Kojima knows her own mind. She discovered her love for Europe at school. A school exchange with Vienna left a lasting impression on her. "The journey was the key to my future." Since then she had dreamt of living in Europe. She was happy in Japan, grew up with a sister in an ordinary family in Tokyo. Still, the European life attracted her an she started a course of German studies at Japan's Reitaku University. During her studies she spent time in Germany, improved her language skills in Halle for two semesters. Bubbling with water she practised the German R. On top of that, she attended language courses at the Berlin Humboldt-University and at the Weimar Bauhaus-Uni.

Satoko's effort helped her to pursue her dream. After her first degree she came to Mecklenburg-Western Pomerania. The German-Japanese society offered her an internship at a company in Rostock. She took the chance and worked in the Japanese Garden at the International Gardening Exhibition (2003). Fascinat-

Satoko Kojima practised saying the German "R" with the aid of water.

ed by her new environment, she decided to do a second degree at Rostock University. In the meantime, the talented linguist is a student assistant and is even learning Low German, a dialect of which not even all the natives have a command. She advises Japanese students, for whom Germany is still literally virgin soil. Despite the financial support by her parents, Satoko works a lot. She runs a work group at a Rostock grammar school, teaches Japanese at the adult education centre and translates websites. Satoko works as an interpreter for the town of Waren, even accompanying a Waren delegation to its twin town Rokkasho as translator in 2005.

Satoko rarely feels homesick. Even though she keeps contact with her parents via e-mail and telephone, she has found a surrogate family here in Mecklenburg-Western Pomerania, who received her warmly when she came to Rostock, and Satoko still spends holidays like Christmas and Easter with her second parents. She also brings a touch of Japanese panache to Mecklenburg. The Japan evening in summer 2005, which Satoko organised with her friends in the main university building, was exciting and unusual for many Rostockers. She herself had not at all expected such a stampede of visitors: 200 guests were wowed by Japanese culture and language. A special quiz taught the surprised participants, that in the Far East beer is as popular as in Germany.

Generally, Japan is very much alike. People do not look for Easter eggs, but at Christmas couples exchange presents as well. "Still, a few things are different", explains Satoko. "In my home country people act conjointly. It is important not to expose others. And Japanese people are more polite." It is even common to take a bow, a tradition that goes back as far as the times of samurai." Satoko admits that she does not like to have her hair cut in Germany. Japanese hairdressers proceeded more cautiously. But these are trifles and do not matter to Satoko.

Studying at Rostock University, Satoko is accompanied by other Japanese students as well. None of them however is rooted as deeply in Germany's soil as is Satoko.

Satoko contributes a great deal to German-Japanese friendship. Some of her fellow countrymen will perhaps be inspired to visit Mecklenburg-Western Pomerania with the aid of the web pages of the tourist board translated by Satoko, and will hopefully be just as interested in the culture of Mecklenburg as the Mecklenburgers are in that of the Far East.

Internet tip: daad.de

Coffee Tradition from Central America

Nicaraguan establishes himself with business idea

Internet tip:
cafeshop-especial.de

The fact that you can find Nicaraguan coffee on breakfast tables throughout Wismar is no longer anything out of the ordinary. This particular coffee, though, has quite a unique history. Javier Román, who runs the coffee shop "Cafeshop Especial" in the Hanseatic City, was born in Nicaragua and has a long tradition of coffee cultivation in his family. His grandfather was an administrator at a large plantation in Central America. All Javier Román knows about coffee, he had learned from him. It was exactly here, where his grandfather had once worked, where Román bought 12,5 hectares of land, in order to cultivate and harvest his own coffee. His entire family would come to him and help him with the harvest. Javier also wants to show his children how much hard work goes into a cup of coffee.

The Román family also experienced hard times in Nicaragua. After Javier met his wife Manuela, a Mecklenburger, at a language course in Moscow, the couple lived together in his homeland. After he had lost his job there, the family decided to resettle in Mecklenburg. Here his childhood dream of coffee finally came true, in the form of a coffee shop, complete with in-store coffee roasting facility. He offers twelve fragrant varieties, all freshly roasted in front of the customers. Javier also sells coffee beans from his own plantations, of course. His home-

The coffee roaster Javier Román harvests some of his coffee for himself.

land should also be able to have a taste of the Nicaraguan's success. He has committed himself to a project, which seeks to help street children there. Román's lucky streak has not yet to come to an end. In the meantime, residents of Rostock are also enjoying the coffee with the unique history. Javier Román has likewise opened a branch here. Franchise owners in Halle and Erfurt are also running successful "Cafeshops Especial".

African wild animals for European courts

Pomeranian taxidermist preserved for eternity

Wild animals to touch, guaranteed safe – taxidermist Carl Knuth offered his clients this unique experience around 1900. They included Prince Heinrich of the Netherlands and various German ducal houses.

Taxidermy came ever more into fashion in the Renaissance, and with the increasing discovery of the world. A real artist in the field of preservation was Carl Knuth from Warnekow near Lassan. He learnt the trade during a lengthy illness, more or less as an autodidact, and made his hobby his profession. He opened an "one-line shop for modern animal preparations" in Schwerin in 1886.

His skill and prominent advocates brought him commissions. The taxidermist also called at courts and received the title of Court Conservator of the Grand Duke of Mecklenburg-Schwerin in 1893. In 1905, Knuth accompanied Duke Adolf Friedrich a trip to Africa, returning with numerous animal preparations. He produced them for example for the Berlin Royal Zoological Museum, as well as for private collections. He also crafted commodities, such as a

Knuth could confidently refer to his title as the supplier to various courts.

Carl Knuth accompanied the journey of Duke Adolf Friedrich to Mecklenburg on the African continent.

table out of rhinoceros parts. Extremely controversial today, they accorded with the prevailing taste of the time. The quality of his work was also esteemed beyond the borders of Mecklenburg. Various ruling houses awarded him court titles. The Grand Duke of Saxony-Weimar-Eisenach and the Duke Regent of Brunswick-Lüneburg made him Court Conservator and Prince Henry of the Netherlands purveyor to the court.

Preserved animals from a German expedition to the South Pole, amazingly lifelike seals, petrels and penguins, earned Knuth the "Grand Prix" and a further prize at the International Oceanography Exhibition in Marseilles in 1906.

Carl Knuth bequeathed his exhibits to the natural history museum in Waren. Now, a mighty red deer prepared by him welcomes visitors at the entrance of today's Müritzeum, a gift by Grand Duke Friedrich Franz IV. The Müritzeum houses a large collection of Knuth's animal preparations as well as the largest aquarium of native freshwater fish in Germany.

Internet tip:
www.mueritzeum.de

Invitation to South Africa

Caspar Venter's homeland thrills Neubrandenburgers

African drums shake the otherwise so peaceful Baltic Sea coast. Namibian beer is served by Caspar Venter. The man from South Africa makes his homeland appetising to the people of Mecklenburg and Western Pomerania with African evenings. With stacks of fascinating pictures and the support of African airline companies and the tourist board, Venter brings the joie de vivre and distinctively colourful and impulsive culture of Africa every year to Woggersin near Neubrandenburg.

He himself has now settled in Mecklenburg-Western Pomerania. He followed his present wife, whom he met while studying in London, to Neubrandenburg in 2001. The 34-year-old cannot quite leave his homeland alone, however, and awakes desire in the people of Mecklenburg and Western Pomerania too for adventure and relaxation in the wilderness of Southern Africa. Caspar and Katja Venter run the Mecklenburg travel company Venter Tours, which organises trips to South Africa, Botswana, Namibia and other countries on the hot continent.

The positive order situation speaks for the cosmopolitanism of the people of Mecklenburg-Western Pomerania. The five members of staff of the only business of its kind in the entire federal state are busy to meet the holiday requirements of all Africa fans.

Internet tip:
www.ventertours.de

Estonians learn from Mecklenburg professor

Rostock pharmacist taught at university in Tartu

In the 19th century many pharmacists and doctors in Russia and the Baltic States studied under the Rostock pharmacist Georg Dragendorff. This scientist was particularly respected in Estonia and Russia, and honours were bestowed on him even in Britain. In London, Georg Dragendorff (1836 -1898) was decorated with the golden Hanbury Medal and at the University of Munich he was awarded an honorary doctorate in Medicine. In Russia he was honoured with the title Council of State. The native of Rostock began his successful international career in 1862 at the St. Petersburg Pharmaceutical Society. In order to retain the talented man from Mecklenburg, he was appointed editor of the "Pharmaceutical Journal for Russia". At the same time, he headed the forensic chemical testing laboratory in St. Petersburg. The University of Dorpat (now Tartu) in Estonia then offered Dragendorff the Chair in Pharmacy. Over a period of 30 years he supervised 90 master's theses in the field of pharmacy and 87 doctoral theses in medicine. His scientific discoveries and their publication in important journals specialising in toxicology, chemistry and pharmacy stimulated progress in these fields and brought Dragendorff international acclaim. The means for

Georg Dragendorff learned the fundamentals of his profession in a Rostock chemist's shop.

Dragendorff's tomb was financed by his "grateful students".

proving the presence of alkaloids, which he discovered, is still called the "Dragendorff reagent".

Before taking up his position at the University of Dorpat, the gifted Dragendorff underwent a course of training at the pharmacy 'Hirsch-Apotheke' in Rostock and then went on to study pharmacy. He later worked in Heidelberg as a laboratory technician. After returning to Rostock he became a research assistant at the Chemical Laboratory there. He was particularly interested in plant analysis and agricultural chemistry.

At the age of 59, after working abroad for 30 years, Georg Dragendorff returned to his hometown, where he died in 1898. Obituaries were published all over Europe. Today, a historic gravestone in the Lindenpark in Rostock stands as a memorial to this important scientist.

Röntgen's teacher and trailblazer in computer technology

Current technology benefits from August Kundt's discoveries

In the 19th century, a physicist from Schwerin made a discovery, whose full scope has only begun to be realized today, in the age of computer technology. The so-called "Kundt-Effect", named after August Kundt, is a magneto-optic phenomenon. Kundt confirmed the rotation of the level of polarisation of light upon its passage through magnetic substances. This phenomenon, combined with laser technology, facilitated today's production of optical storage.

Paper-thin metal film, which computer technology is inseparable from, has its origins in a discovery made by Kundt. He produced it for the first time in 1886, with the help of cathodic sputtering.

August Kundt led a short, but scientifically extremely successful life.

His accomplishments within the realms of physics and mathematics were gained at the University of Leipzig. By virtue of his brilliant achievements, Kundt was hired as a professor at the polytechnic institute in Zurich in 1868. After his professorship in Würzburg, Kundt relocated to Strassburg in 1872, where he directed the construction of the Physics Institute at the newly founded university there. He was then appointed rector some six years later. Kundt had almost 50 scientific works published, he discovered the characteristics of mercury vapor, and conducted research in various fields such as optics, electricity and the study of crystals. He was appointed to Berlin sixteen years later. His shining reputation preceded him, so that he could hardly deal with the enormous inflow of students. One of his students was the then six years younger Conrad Röntgen, who was later awarded the first Nobel Prize for physics in 1901.

Kundt had dedicated himself totally to science, and was a member of the academy, various societies and clubs and wrote as the editor for the journal 'Advancement of Physics'. His industrious life was seriously impaired by heart disease, from which he was never able to recover. Kundt died at the age of only 54 in May of 1894 in Israeldorf, near Lübeck.

Internet tip:
www.en.wikipedia.org

Pursuing migratory birds by bike

Otto Steinfatt followed migratory birds all the way to Africa

The Mecklenburg man Otto Steinfatt pursued migratory birds with his bike to the Bosporus, to Sicily and Spain, in order to find out, where they fly to and how they breed. His thirst for knowledge led him all the way to North Africa. Steinfatt pitched his tent in Morocco, Tunisia, Libya, Switzerland, Poland, Hungary, Greece, and also on the Canary Islands, Malta, in Bulgaria, Romania, Turkey, Scandinavia and also in the Baltic countries. Otto Steinfatt from Wittenförden is regarded as a trailblazer of modern ornithology. He was one of the first people to receive colour film from European film producers Afga, already before the Second World War. He used the film for his photographic documentation and made extraordinary photographs. Steinfatt described the breeding habits of 37 types of bird in great detail in his published works. Ornithologists still refer back to his works and photos even today.

Steinfatt was constantly travelling by bike, because of the lack of funds for more comfortable transportation. Compelled by his interest in the details of bird migration, the natural scientist travelled virtually through every single country in Europe.

Born in Jamel and raised near Schwerin in the Mecklenburg countryside, his love for nature was essentially a forgone conclusion. With the

Internet tip:
www.wittenfoerden.de

The bicycle played a central role in Otto Steinfatt's work.

help of a scholarship, he was able to finance his studies of natural sciences in Innsbruck, Vienna, Berlin, Munich and Freiburg. The areas in which he studied were used as a starting point for his travels. In 1935, Otto Steinfatt was employed in the forest station for pest control in the Romint Heath in what is today Poland. Thanks to his research, the forestry service was about to keep harmful insects at bay. Later he worked as a teacher in the School for Forestry of Raben Steinfeld near Schwerin. On 1st May 1947, Steinfatt suffered a violent death in Mecklenburg. Because of his reluctance to hand over his bicycle to a stranger, he was killed.

Gateways to the world

International air traffic in Mecklenburg-Western Pomerania

One state president after another strides along the red carpet towards the airport terminal building. However, the airport in question is not that of Berlin or New York but the regional airport of Mecklenburg-Western Pomerania, Rostock-Laage. In June 2007, the heads of state of the world's most powerful economies were welcomed by Prime Minister Harald Ringstorff before travelling on to the G8 Summit at Heiligendamm.

The airport in Laage, to the south of the Hanseatic City of Rostock, has provided passenger services to domestic and international destinations since 1993. In the intervening years, the former military airbase has developed into an important hub in the north of Germany. Charter flights take tourists to Hungary, Egypt or Greece. Every year, around 180,000 people take advantage of the services provided in the modern terminal building, which opened in 2005.

After the reunification of Germany, the Bundeswehr took over the airbase, but in 1992 a contract for civilian use of the base was concluded. A year later, about 60 hectares out of a total area of 1,000 hectares were released for civilian use. This collaboration between military and civilian operators is unique in the German air traffic system. Since 2004, the Bundeswehr has been using the base for training flights with its Eurofighter planes. From 1995

Internet tips:
www.rostock-airport.de
www.airport-parchim.de
www.flughafen-neubrandenburg.de

The French President Nicholas Sarkosy has also already landed at Rostock Laage.

until 2005, Rostock-Laage was also part of the night-flight network of the German postal service, Deutsche Post AG.

But the airport is not Mecklenburg-Western Pomerania's only gateway to the world. Planes carrying tourists to Bulgaria, Greece and Turkey also regularly take off from Parchim and Neubrandenburg-Trollenhagen. In future, Parchim Airport will also have special connections to the Far East. The Chinese company Link Global Logistics took over the airport in May 2007. This is the first time that a Chinese company has obtained an operating licence for a European airport. As well as conducting cargo flights from the Central Chinese city of Zhengzhou, which has a population of around 7 million, the investor is also considering establishing a weekly passenger service. Then you might hear announcements in a Chinese departure lounge saying: "Passengers travelling to Mecklenburg-Western Pomerania are requested to proceed to the gate."

Sternberg man revolutionised German shipping

First iron screw steamship was launched on the river Warnow

The Sternberger Albrecht Tischbein revolutionised German shipbuilding with ideas from Holland and England. He built Germany's first iron ships in Rostock, thereby leading the country into the age of modern shipbuilding. The shipbuilding pioneer learned from his forerunners in Holland and England, whose shipbuilding had changed fundamentally with industrialisation. Iron began to catch on as shipbuilding material, above all in Great Britain. In Rotterdam, Tischbein worked together with Gerhard Moritz Roentgen, the eminent Dutch officer and shipbuilder.

Tischbein was born in Sternberg in 1803 and grew up in Rostock. From 1822, he studied in the Netherlands, where he later supervised the construction of steamships as engineer. He gained experience here and during his stay in England, which he later applied in his homeland. In 1850, he presented a special project in Rostock: the building of an iron steamship. Shipbuilders had been using wood as the most important working material for over three thousand years, and this had also been the raw material used by Rostock shipbuilders up to that point to build seagoing vessels.

Together with the master shipbuilder Wilhelm Zeltz, he set up the first Rostock iron shipyard, and the engineers were commissioned to build two iron screw steamships. One year later, Al-

Albrecht Tischbein focused on iron, the modern raw-material.

brecht Tischbein brought German ocean shipping the breakthrough. The first seaworthy screw steam-ship of riveted iron, named the "Erbgroßherzog Friedrich Franz", was launched in Rostock. Its sister ship, the "Großfürst Constantin", followed a year later.

Albrecht Tischbein died in March 1881. The shipyard founded by Tischbein later became the Rostock Neptun shipyard, which still operates in the maritime sector today. Iron shipbuilding, thanks to the Sternberger Tischbein, boosted the entire German shipbuilding industry and its maritime trade. Incidentally, the engineer Tischbein did not just build ships, but also constructed gas preparation plants and steam pumps for locomotives.

English style seaside resort

International history of Heiligendamm

"Heic te laetitia invitat post balnea sanum"- You are invited to enjoy yourself here after a healing bath. By this charming invitation the white town by the sea has attracted innumerable guests from home and abroad for more than 200 years. The unquestioned peak of its history marked the the G8 Summit in 2007. The heads of government of the eight leading industrial nations resided where even the Russian Tsar once was a guest.

Mecklenburg-Western Pomerania owes this gem of a place to Frederick-Francis I Duke of Mecklenburg Schwerin, who took his first bath in the Baltic Sea at Heiligen Damm in 1793. Not so much because of the curing water, but rather to boost his duchy's economic upturn, he got enthusiastic about the establishment of a public seaside resort. Following the great English examples of Brighton and Bath he caused the erection of white, elegant houses along the cost and thus created the first German seaside resort.

Half a century later, Grand Duke Paul Frederick made the resort a real summer residence. Until 1865 graceful villas were built, placed along the coast like pearls on a string. From that time on visitors remembered the bright ensemble of houses as "white town by the sea". No less than the European high nobility including the prince royal of Prussia, Field Marshal Blücher, Wilhelm von Humboldt and the

Further reading:
B. Schümann /
T. Grundner, Heiligendamm, Rostock 2006

Heiligendamm, "the white town by the sea", impresses with its architecture.

Tsar's family were among them. The exclusive seaside resort became increasingly popular until the 1930s. During national socialism, however, only those took a bath at Heiligendamm, who were allowed to according to German race ideologists. After the Second World War many patients were welcomed to Heiligendamm's bathhouses and villas then functioning as sanatoriums and convalescent homes.

In 1996, a group of investors named Fundus purchased the white town by the sea. Due to extensive renovations it celebrates its glorious renaissance today. The Kempinski Grand Hotel Heiligendamm opened in spring 2003 and welcomes visitors to its fashionable apartments and meeting rooms. As luxurious as ever the exclusive spa receives international guests looking for recreation. Still joy invites them after healing baths: Starred chefs surprise gourmets with delicious meals.

Internet tip:
www.bad-doberan.de

Rostock family in Europe and overseas

An emigrant story of the 19th century

In the year 1692, a young man by the name of Hinrich Krahnstöver came from Hamburg to Rostock. For seven generations, the family lived in the Hanseatic City on the Warnow, playing a decisive role in Rostock's industry. A gravestone in the St Marien church remembers Hinrich and his grandson, master furrier Johann Andreas Krahnstöver. One of the best known members of the family is the liqueur manufacturer Julius Krahnstöver. And two Krahnstövers bore their name into the wide world. Rostock Captain Gottfried Krahnstöver and his wife Wilhelmine had four children. The eldest son, Wilhelm Paul, was born on 14 August 1831 and went to England while still a young man. Thanks to his wife's relatives in Stettin, father Gottfried had built up intensive business relations in the United Kingdom and himself called several times at English ports in his ship.

Now Wilhelm Paul was able to make use of this. He received sound commercial training and was sent to East India to trade on behalf of England. He concluded scores of excellent contracts and did lucrative business in the indigo trade. The Rostock lad Wilhelm Paul became a wealthy overseas trader and globetrotter, and took English citizenship, henceforth calling himself William. Houses owned in London, Calcutta, Baden-Baden and Florence bear witness to his wealth. On 30th September 1868, he married Berthe Clara Bianca Sommier, who subsequently germanised her name to Bertha Sommer. She was the daughter of a no less well off jeweller from the Alsace. William Krahnstöver died in 1922.

Collector's items from the Krahnstöver house in Florence are kept in the Uffizi galleries and in the Florence Ethnographic Museum. Today, there are descendants living in Switzerland and Alsace, as well as Leipzig, Celle and St Goar.

The second Krahnstöver to venture abroad was Ernst Albert Friedrich Krahnstöver, who was

The branch of the family which emigrated to the USA supported itself through the dyeing and cleaning trades.

born on 13th March 1846 in the living quarters above the business premises of his father's house in the Rostock Hopfenmarkt. His father would have indeed liked to have seen Ernst become a goldsmith like himself. But the young man had other interests. He wanted to become a chemist. The trade of dyer, in which of course chemistry plays its part, was a compromise. The 16-year-old Ernst began his apprenticeship, subsequently went on walkabout and finally, in 1869, started a business in the parental house.

One year later, he established himself with his own business in Schwerin. But that could not keep him there for long. After his father's early death, he decided to return to his home town. 32 years old, he met his future wife Louise. They married on 31st May 1878 and had children.

So the master dyer's family lived until the year that changed everything: 1889, when they decided to emigrate to America. In contrast to others, the standard of life was not the reason for departure. As Ernst Krahnstöver later recounted, it was rather that he on no account wished to send his sons to the military. They should serve neither under the Grand Duke nor under the Kaiser.

The Krahnstöver family started its voyage across the ocean in June 1889. After a stop in Bremen, where the America emigrants were looked after, the journey continued by train to Bremerhaven. At the emigrant quay, the Fulda, built in Glasgow at John Elder & Co. in 1882, was expecting them. As well as the married couple Louise and Ernst Krahnstöver, the five children, between three and ten years of age, were on board the fast steamship.

Brother-in-law Adolf Dernehl was waiting for the newcomers in New York. He also signed the immigration papers. Louise's brothers, Adolf, Ulrich and William, had already been in the States since 1882. Adolf was a grocery trader and already had his business on a firm footing. He saw the conditions as favourable for Ernst too. First, they travelled together by train to Milwaukee. The city in the State of Wisconsin was to be the new home of the Rostockers. Shortly after their arrival, a special event was the birth of Harry, the first Krahn-

> The family dachshund also came along as a stowaway – illegally, as the children did not want to be separated from their "Pussel".

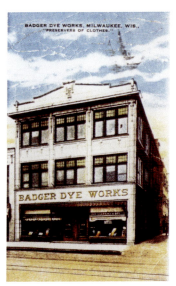

Ernst Krahnstöver's second business house in Milwaukee

stöver to be born in the States. Emigrants from Germany had settled principally in Cincinnati, St. Louis and Milwaukee. Milwaukee then had 250,000 inhabitants, and a large German quarter. It was virtually a prerequisite here that business people were proficient in the German language. Americanisation only became established around 1930.

With his own means and with investments by his brother-in-law, Ernst Krahnstöver rapidly built up a livelihood. In North Avenue, in the heart of the German quarter, he established the dyeing and cleaning business "Badger Dye Works". Soon after this he was able to buy out four competitors, making him the largest service provider in his branch of trade in Milwaukee. He specialised in fireproof curtains. In 1907, Ernst Krahnstöver started to build up a second business.

The Krahnstöver children went to school until the eighth grade and grew up bilingual. However, in view of his increasing deafness, it was not given to father Ernst to learn English. Thus mother Louise dealt with all the business transactions in English. The business ran well beyond the life of Ernst Krahnstöver until the Great Depression (1929-1941), after which it never really recovered. The house was to be sold by the family in 1963.

Vietnamese ambassador in Bad Doberan

County town exports marine technology all over the world

Vessels all over the world are fitted out with ventilation, refrigeration and air-conditioning systems by a company from Bad Doberan. Why do foreign shipyards buy technology from a little town on the Baltic coast? The business from Mecklenburg-Western Pomerania has now developed into a true global player. Selck GmbH & Co. KG from Bad Doberan manufactures and supplies products for shipyards in Vietnam, China, and the USA, as well as for private customers in every corner of the world. It fitted out the popular Aida Club ships with its own patented state-of-the-art pipe connections for the fire-extinguishing system, which are currently unrivalled anywhere in the world. As well as in Bad Doberan, the company has manufacturing facilities in Philadelphia (USA) and in Hai Phong (Vietnam). The Vietnamese Ambassador, Tran Duc Mau, even paid a personal visit to the Selck Group in Bad Doberan, in 2006. The company recently opened a branch in Singapore which specialises in sales and services.

The family business was established in 1993 with just ten employees. Now it employs a workforce of 250.

Internet tip:
www.sht-deutschland.de

From left to right: Daniel Selck, Trung Hieu, Ambassador Tran Duc Mau, Deputy Chief of Mission Nguyen Minh Gon, and Harald Selck in Bad Doberan

Christmas parcels from Sweden

Jangling presents for the neighbours

"Huuch Julklapp!" comes the unexpected cry out of the background, then there's a thud and the door bangs shut. Looking for the cause of the noise with a scared face, one comes upon a packet with a note attached with one's own name on it and whose form appears strange. But the addressee knows this pre-Christmas game. He tries to tear open the tightly tied packaging and ultimately gets to another sealed packet, addressed to someone from the nearby area. Now the receiver, likewise unremarked, must throw this packet into the house of the target person, while loudly crying "Huuch Julklapp" and disappear as fast as possible before he is discovered. In this way the packet can change hands several more times and finally land up with the person whose name last adorns the packaging. The fun however is not for the person receiving but for the person giving the present, namely because of the disappointment over the ultimate appearance of strange or ugly objects. For this reason, Julklapp was an opportunity for practical jokes and badinage, particularly among the young. These goings-on did the rounds of the villages of Mecklenburg and Pomerania like a pre-Christmas spook. And it was a dyed-in-the-wool cultural import from Sweden. In Sweden itself, the custom emerged at the end of the 17th century, making its way to Mecklenburg and Western Pomerania through the active trade contacts and the Swedish occupation from 1648 to 1815. And although "Julklapp throwing" has largely disappeared today, it was well-known all over Pomerania, on Rügen and Usedom into the 1930s. The first evidence for the custom of Julklappen in the region is to be found as early as the early 20s and 30s of the 19th century.

"Julklapp" was a popular Christmas custom up to the 1930s.

"Julklappen" is derived from the Swedish "klappa pa dören" (knock on the door). The custom also came to be slightly modified in the course of time. Thus later, in some places, the packets were handed over in the party room on Christmas Eve and adorned with clues for seeking the actual present rather than changing addressees. Frequently, presentees found their gifts in the garden or even in the hen-coop then. The function of the custom remained unaltered thereby; Julklapp was supposed to bring humour and caprice into the otherwise rather contemplative festival. As the parlours of the ever smaller families became ever more cosy and prosperous in the age of industrialisation and neighbourhood relationships broke down, the Swedish custom slowly got lost. Still, Christmas presents will never go out of fashion; so why not liven up Julklapp and give presents to neighbours merrily and loudly.

Rostock woman governed Russia

Anna Leopoldovna and the tsardom

A woman of Rostock ruled the Tsarist Empire. Not a Russian fairytale, but the true story of Anna Leopoldovna (1718-1746). In the 18th century, the daughter of the Hanseatic City became Grand Duchess and Regent. The daughter of Duke Karl Leopold of Mecklenburg and Katharina Ivanova the niece of Tsarina Anna Ivanova. She was born in Rostock as Elisabeth Katharina Christine on 18th December 1718.

Karl Leopold resided in Schwerin Castle, in the present-day regional capital of Mecklenburg-Western Pomerania. Political difficulties in the Mecklenburg-Schwerin of that time, however, caused him to flee with his family to Gdansk. Katharina Ivanovna left the town for Russia with Elisabeth in 1722.

The sister of the Duchess, Anna Ivanovna, ruling Russian Tsarina from 1729, prepared her niece for life at court. Elisabeth received an excellent education, joined the Russian Orthodox Church and took the name "Anna Leopoldovna". As the Tsarina had no offspring herself, she saw her succession as assured through the expected progeny of the Rostock woman. But the throne of the Tsars also awoke concupiscence in others.

The Austrian Empress in Vienna married her nephew Ulrich von Brunswick to Anna Leopoldovna in 1739 to consolidate relations between the noble houses of Brunswick-Wolfenbüttel and Romanov and thus of Austria and Russia. Anna Leopoldovna bore her son Ivan in 1740.

The incumbent Tsarina Anna Ivanovna wished to secure the regency for her favourite, Count Biron. She therefore appointed the underage Ivan as her successor in 1740 and Biron as his guardian. But her favourite was overthrown, and Anna Leopoldovna, the former Rostock girl Elisabeth, ensured herself of the regency in the same year as Grand Duchess. Elisabeth Petrovna, aunt of the Rostock woman, soon intervened in the conflicts for the throne. The conspirators overthrew Anna Leopoldovna in 1741, in the night from 5th to 6th December. Elisabeth Petrovna, daughter of Peter the Great, finally ascended to the Russian throne as Elisabeth I. Anna Leopoldovna and her lord were exiled to Cholmogory on the Dvina. Their son Ivan was imprisoned in the dungeon of the Fortress of Schlüsselburg near St. Petersburg and murdered there in 1764.

Anna Leopoldowna was overthrown by conspirators in 1741.

Peter I apprenticed near Lake Müritz

Tsar learned blacksmith's craft at castle near Röbel

Peter I travelled through Europe in his search for innovations.

Peter the Great was a man of action. Anxious to redress the backwardness of his own country, the ambitious ruler travelled westwards in 1697/98 with the aim of fathoming the secrets of the European naval powers. Accompanied by 200 lords, artisans, servants and musicians, he perambulated Western Europe to learn techniques of use in building a state power to be taken seriously. As Peter Mikhailov, he had Prussian cannons explained to him in Königsberg, learned about Dutch shipbuilding techniques at an Amsterdam shipyard and found out about astronomy and medicine in England. Even a small village in Mecklenburg-Western Pomerania proudly remembers having taught the great Emperor something. In Wredenhagen Castle near Röbel, Peter I is supposed to have learnt the craft of the blacksmith en route for the Netherlands. The ruler was clearly a diligent student, for during his reign the Russian empire advanced to become a world power.

Still today, eager pupils study at Wredenhagen Castle: at a primary school. Also, against a mediaeval backdrop, lovers of majestic birds of prey can observe hunting scenes at the castle as in the times of Peter the Great.

Rostock rector in Canadian gown

Thomas Strothotte remembered his roots at inauguration

The Alma Mater Rostochiensis welcomed a very special "freshman" for the winter semester 2006/2007. A born-and-bred Canadian contested his first semester at the oldest university in North Germany (founded in 1419), not as a visiting student or the like, but as the new rector. Thomas Strothotte defiled through the Hanseatic City in his Canadian gown from the main building in Universitätsplatz to St. Marien church – accompanied by professors, students and sightseers on 2nd October 2006. The computer scientist changed his robe just before the ceremony of investiture.

The 47-year was elected as the new vice-chancellor at the University council for a term of office from 2006 to 2010 in May 2006. Born in Regina in Saskatchewan, Canada, the professor of computer science studied Physics and Computer Science in Vancouver, worked in Montreal, Ontario and Paris, qualified as a professor in Stuttgart and was appointed at the Free University of Berlin. From 1993, Strothotte was professor of Computer Science at Magdeburg University.

Since 2006 the office of Rostock Rector has been held by a Canadian.

Now, the new university boss wants to strengthen international partnerships with Canadian multi-culture and German dependability and expand and exploit the role of the largest university in Mecklenburg-Western Pomerania as a gateway to the world.

State funeral for Argentina explorer

Stralsund scholar worked in South America

Many are the achievements of a Stralsund man: a zoologist, geographer, geologist, botanist, ornithologist, palaeontologist and meteorologist of international reputation. He criss-crossed his adopted country, Argentina, discovering, describing, sketching, collecting and tabulating virtually innumerable finds.

Already as a schoolboy, Carl Hermann Conrad Burmeister (1807-1892) attracted attention – his great abilities amazed all his teachers. They supported his great interest in beetles and butterflies and recommend him for a course of studies at Greifswald University. After his final examination in 1825, he enrolled for his doctorate at the science faculty. Two years later, he went to Halle on the Saale river to learn from luminaries of zoology, botany, palaeontology and medicine at the university. By 1829, the high-flying scientist received his doctorates at the faculties of medicine and philosophy and henceforth enthused students with his lively lectures.

Burmeister's friendship with Alexander von Humboldt smoothed his way to Berlin university, where he became a professor in 1834. Three years later, Halle appointed him back as a full professor. Besides, he assiduously populated the collections of the city's Zoological Museum with exhibits.

Thanks to the advocacy of Alexander von Humboldt, the Stralsunder journeyed to the

South American tropics a number of times from 1850. From this time on, the richly populated nature of the subcontinent never released its hold on the natural scientist and, in 1861, he finally relocated fully to Buenos Aires. Here, the professor was honoured with the post of Director of the Museo Publico. Thanks to his commitment, the institute blossomed out in the following 30 years under his guidance into a famous establishment. The director worked tirelessly and maked the museum famous beyond the borders of the country. On numerous expeditions all over South America he described countless unknown animal and plant species. Many of his discoveries, including a peak on Spitzbergen, bear his name. He studied his adopted country diligently until the material was sufficient for an entire applied geography of Argentina. The list of his scientific publications is however far longer: the scholar's work comprises approximately 300 titles. He assiduously wrote down and sketched his impressions for posterity. But the adoptive Argentinean did not merely describe flora and fauna, but also criticised political abuses, such as the omnipresent slavery. The man from Western Pomerania enjoyed equally high regard as scientific advisor to the Argentinean government as he did as a scientist. The country's president himself commissioned him to set up a science faculty at the University of Cordoba.

When the great scientist died at the age of eighty-five in 1892, all Argentina honoured his merits with a state funeral.

Carl Hermann Conrad was fascinated by South America.

Internet tip:
www.meeres
museum.de

Mecklenburg's name for Maderia's souvenir

Keepsake owes its name to Mecklenburg-Strelitz

Strictly speaking, every tourist who buys a souvenir of Maderia and of Trinidad and Tobago also buys a memento from Mecklenburg-Western Pomerania. The so-called bird-of-paradise flower is the perfect souvenir to take a piece of sun-drenched vacation back home. Securely packed in wooden cases, countless numbers are taken from the vacation islands to the far reaches of the earth in tourist's luggage. Many buyers of the souvenir regard the West Indies as the home of this charming plant, whose blossom resembles the headdress of the magnificent bird of paradise. Its story begins, however, on the complete opposite end of the world.

In fact, the bird-of-paradise flower has its origins on the sweltering continent of Africa. In the year 1772, the plant collector Francis Masson discovered the paradisical Musaceae on the Cape of Good Hope. Masson, along with seafarer James Cook, was sent to South Africa by order of the famous scientist and botanist Joseph Banks. Banks, for his part, was a member of the Royal Society and therefore directly answerable to the crown. The queen of the British Empire at that time, Queen Charlotte, took a great interest in botany and fully supported Bank's endeavour. The scientist appeared exceedingly impressed by the gorgeous flower and named it, in honour of his Queen of botany, "strelitzia reginae", in accordance with the Queen's ancestry. Queen Charlotte, the so-called "Queen of botany", descended from the house of Mecklenburg-Strelitz, and in 1761, was married to the British King George III. Queen Charlotte let her family in Mecklenburg-Strelitz take part in her enjoyment by

presenting her homeland with a shrub of the plant as a gift. Four years later the plant blossomed for the first time on German soil. In 1995, the town of Neustrelitz, the former residence of the Grand Duchy of Mecklenburg-Strelitz, named the strelitzia reginae the official flower of the city. Thus visitors to Madeira, by their paradisical mementos, bring home not only a reminder of their vacation, but also a piece of Mecklenburg-Western Pomerania.

The strelitzia flower recalls the former Duchy of Mecklenburg-Strelitz.

Flags from the King

Mecklenburg dynasty in Danish service

Ludorf Manor House is considered one of the oldest and loveliest in Mecklenburg-Western Pomerania. It was built in the style of the Danish Clinker Renaissance by order of Adam Levin von Knuth, who was closely connected with Denmark.

His father, Jakob Ernst Knuth, of the most ancient Mecklenburg noble lineage and lord of the manor of Leizen, Melz and Priborn, was in the Danish service as cavalry captain and had acquired Ludorf through marriage. Adam Levin and his younger brother Eggert Christoffer were already pages at the court of the Danish king as boys and grew up bosom friends to the heir to the throne, Christian V. Adam Levin later acquired the important position of royal chamberlain, roughly corresponding to that of today's prime minister. Eggert Christoffer founded the noble Knuth line on the Jutland peninsula. Through marriage to Søster Lerche he acquired estates on Lolland. Their son Adam Christoffer Knuth founded what is today the Knuthenborg Safari Park, the best known of its kind in Northern Europe, with his wife Charlotte.

In 1689, Adam inherited the estate in his homeland Mecklenburg and built the manor house,

The entrance to the Ludorf farmhouse shows the family coat-of-arms of the von Knuths.

which still radiates a lordly air today. What it lacks in decoration outside is more than made up for by the interior décor. Baroque ceiling frescoes bear witness to Adam Levin's artistry. The Knuth coat of arms, a pot-hanger with three clover leaves, crowns the entrance. The Knuths likewise have King Christian V to thank for the three red flags. The King complemented the clover leaves with the flags at the end of the 17th century. Both branches of the family, in Mecklenburg and Denmark, recognised the extended national emblem and continued to use it.

Since 1998, the new owners of the manor and outbuilding have been the Achtenhagen family. Since 2002, the ancient country estate functions as country house hotel.

Internet tip:
www.gutshaus-ludorf.de

Today the house is used as a hotel.

Artworks from Güstrow in the Far East

Works by Ernst Barlach exhibited in Japan

In 1927, this Barlach portrait was done by Emil Orlik.

Museums in Kyoto, Tokyo and Kofu showed the comprehensive retrospective "Ernst Barlach. The Sculptor of German Expressionism" from 20th February to 17th July 2006 as part of the German Year 2005/2006. Sculptures, prints, drawings and other artworks made their journey to the land of the rising sun on the initiative of the former German Ambassador to Japan, Henrik Schmiegelow. Although, for centuries, Japan gave little heed to occidental culture, the artistic creation of Ernst Barlach has found its way into Japanese culture and is held in high esteem here.

Ernst Barlach (1870-1938) is among the most important artists of German modernity. His unmistakable style, reducing the bodies of his figures to the essentials, was evolved by Ernst Barlach in his adopted home of Güstrow in Mecklenburg. Born in Wedel near Hamburg, he studied sculpture in Dresden and Paris. He changed his place of domicile several times between Berlin and Hamburg, searching for his artistic signature. He overcame his inner unrest and artistic creative crisis on a trip to Russia around 1906. The primitiveness of Russia and the hard life of the simple people were important experiences for him. In Güstrow, Barlach rediscovered his power, set up a studio and started work again.

Germany's voice in the concert of nations

Gunter Pleuger represented Germany at the UN

He was Germany's man at the heart of the world's action: Mecklenburger Gunter Pleuger. His career began with a dream job. In 1970, one year after he commenced his duties at the Foreign Office, the man from Wismar was sent to New York. He was a member of the German observation mission at UNO, until both German states were admitted as members of the United Nations in 1973. "It was an incredibly exciting appointment in a period of upheaval, when Germany once more had to and was allowed to take a stronger stand in political events", says Pleuger.

Gunter Pleuger was born in the Hanseatic Town of Wismar in 1941. In 1945, the family moved to Westphalia. Despite the division of Germany, Pleuger remained in contact with friends and relations in Wismar. Before his diplomatic career, he had studied and graduated in law and political science in Cologne and Bonn. He attended the École Nationale d'Administration (ENA) in Paris for a year. As well as his first assignment in the Federal Republic mission at the United Nations, the Foreign Office assigned him to the German embassies in New Delhi and Washington. Thereafter he made a career in Bonn and Berlin, as head of the UNO and human rights department and as State Secretary of the Foreign Office among others. As to the question of his homeland, he responds by naming Europe, Germany and Wismar alike – according to one's point of view. Three places are however not enough for this cosmopolitan. As interested as he is in his own culture, he is enthusiastic about those of foreign countries as well. East Asian culture for instance fascinates him with the 5,000-year history which its architecture and language recount.

At the end of his career, Pleuger went back once more to New York. He ended his diplomatic career where had begun it. From 2002 to 2006, he was Germany's Permanent Representative among the 192 countries of UNO. The controversy about the Iraq crisis and Germany's two-year membership of the Security Council once more demanded a great deal of sensitive handling from Pleuger. His opposition to Washington's policy of war left a lasting impression, not only in the USA.

After four decades of service at the Foreign Office, he still holds, as a retired diplomat, an ambassadorial post: as the delegate of his Mecklenburg homeland. True to his philosophy "carpe diem" he is involved in the Pro MV initiative, which uses prominent personalities to promote the federal state. Pleuger plugs Mecklenburg-Western Pomerania in guest lectures, as he says, to help to bring the state to international attention after the G8 Summit has ended. In private, he also remains loyal to the north-east: the Pleugers continue to celebrate big family parties in Wismar, and the annual holiday on Rügen is equally obligatory.

Internet tip:
www.mv-tut-gut.de

With a wheelbarrow across Kamchatka

Two Rostock adventurers do extreme sports all over the world

By bicycle around the world. – Ronald Prokein and Markus Möller from Rostock have cycled round the whole globe. They have trekked across Asia, paddled through rapids in Siberia in simple kayaks, and toured the Russian taiga in a truck. These Rostock adventurers have survived freezing temperatures, violent thunderstorms and torrential rains of biblical proportions. On foot and with a wheelbarrow as a rather unusual item of baggage, they have even dared to travel 1,000 kilometres across the Russian volcanic peninsula of Kamchatka.

Markus Möller and Ronald Prokein want to explore the world independently. A car journey to southern Europe aroused their thirst for adventure, and just two years later, in 1993, they began their first real quest: to drive by car through the Sahara.

Their next enterprise was a cycling trip. 18,000 kilometres in 161 days. On a tour of Asia they even planned to pay a visit to the Sultan of Brunei. It turned out to be a real adventure: having had a car accident in the middle of Russia, they had to travel on in an extremely rickety goods train, and then they went bankrupt in a Russian casi-

Möller and Prokein walked across the Kamtschatka peninsula with wheelbarrows.

no. Yet the adventurers did not give up, managing to make their way through Japan, Brunei, Pakistan and China without any money.

In the year 2000 the globetrotters paddled through Siberia in kayaks for 47 days. They experienced more than 3,000 kilometres of oppressive heat, freezing cold and isolation in the Russian taiga.

After having tried out every means of transportation they took the next challenge: a wheelbarrow instead of a rucksack. The two men pushed their luggage over 1,000 kilometres across Kamchatka. The earth quaked beneath their feet, they climbed vulcanos and they were eyeball-to-eyeball with brown bears.

Ronald Prokein set off once again in January 2004: this time to Ojmjakon, the coldest place in the world. Again he returned safe and sound. From May to August 2006, the 34-year-old ran more than 5,000 kilometres from Istanbul to the North Cape. At the same time, his colleague Markus Möller was again in Siberia, walking as far as his feet would carry him. He was tracing the footsteps of Clemens Forell, the story of whose amazing escape through Asia is told in the film of the similar title 'As Far as My Feet will Carry Me'. Ronald Prokein set off for Siberia once again in December 2007: this time to Jutschjugej, a village near Ojmjakon.

Internet tip:
www.aufbrechen.de

Silver Condor flew to the end of the world

Pilot with Mecklenburg roots explores Tierra del Fuego

He felt as a Mecklenburger and named Schwerin his home town: the aviation pioneer pioneer, seafarer, writer, filmmaker and explorer Gunther Plüschow (1886-1931), who was the first person to fly over the fantastic scenery of Tierra del Fuego in the legendary Silver Condor, a biplane from Rostock.

Born in Munich, he spent the first years of his childhood in Rome. From 1895, the Plüschow family lived in Mecklenburg, where they originated from. Gunther Plüschow's grandfather Eduard was an illegitimate (but acknowledged) child of the hereditary Grand Duke Friedrich-Ludwig of Mecklenburg-Schwerin.

At the age of 10 he started a military career, according to an old family tradition. In the cadet school however, he felt trapped and yearned for the freedom of Tierra del Fuego, which he knew from photos and stories.

His lust for adventure took him as a flyer of the German Imperial Marines to the fortress at Tsingtao (China). When Japanese troops besieged the fortress in 1914, he managed to break out of the city in spectacular fashion in his plane. After nine months of flight through China, the USA and England, he reached home in July 1915, becoming famous as the legendary "flyer of Tsingtao".

Plüschow set out for his dream goal, Tierra del Fuego, in November 1927, at the age of 41.

In 1928 Plüschow began a flight over Tierra del Fuego with this aircraft.

A simple fishing cutter, converted into a research ship, brought the adventurer and his team to the end of the world. Also en route: a biplane, the Heinkel HD 24 W seaplane – well packed onto a steamer and well locked after by the engineer Ernst Dreblow.

Plüschow's team assembled the component parts at a shipyard in Punta Arenas in Chile and the pilot took off on his first great flight from Punta Arenas, Chile, to Ushuaia, Argentina – across the big island of Tierra del Fuego. He had a postbag with him and thus almost incidentally delivered the first air mail from Punta Arenas to Ushuaia.

Plüschow and his flight engineer Ernst Dreblow, in their biplane, the "Silver Condor" were the first people to hover over the Cordillera Darwin on the Isla Grande de Tierra del Fuego, Cape Horn and Torres del Paine in Patagonia. Fascinated by the overwhelming beauty of the inland Patagonian ice, the explorers for the first time brought back photos and film material from these previously unexplored regions of South America. The book "Silver Condor over Tierra del Fuego" became an early bestseller and gave many amazed readers their first glimpse of Tierra del Fuego and Patagonia.

To fill in the final blank spaces on the map, Plüschow and Dreblow started afresh for South America in July 1930. But this time, the Silver Condor did not bring them back. On 28th January 1931, the explorers tragically crashed their Heinkel biplane into the icy waters of Lake Rico.

The legendary "Tsingtao flyer" brought spectacular pictures with him from his journey.

Chile and Argentina still commemorate Plüschow today. The aviation pioneer was most recently honoured on 12th December 2006 with a square in Punta Arenas being named after him. In October 2007, a ceremony was held in his honour in the Argentine Parliament. In Germany, the "Freundeskreis Gunther Plüschow" feels obliged to preserve the memory of the aviation pioneer. The members remind of life and work of this extraordinary personality with articles, lectures and exhibitions.

Internet tip:
Gunther-Plueschow.de

Honoured on the moon

Friedrich von Hahn's merits perpetuated in space

He may not have strolled on the moon like Neil Armstrong and Edwin Aldrin, but Friedrich von Hahn (1742-1805) also made such a giant leap for mankind that he has even been eternalised on the earth's satellite.

The humanist was one of the pioneers who spread the ideas of the Enlightenment in Mecklenburg. He used simple means, for instance had a school built where only trained staff taught. Remplin Castle between Malchin and Teterow served him as a chemical laboratory for some scientific experiments. Here he also mounted a laboratory and a collection of physical instruments.

One of his passions was astronomy. From 1793 to 1805, Hahn operated an observatory at Remplin. In 1791, he had his summerhouse converted into an observatory without international equal. The construction was distinguished by a revolving astrodome, of which there were only a few in the whole of Europe. Hahn's reflecting telescope was one of the most modern and largest in the world. With extensive instruments, he observed planet surfaces, the physical nature of the sun and nebular objects, and discovered the

In its time the observatory in Remplin was among the most modern in Europe.

central star in the Ring Nebula in the constellation Lyra. His sometimes novel approaches were published by the astronomer in 20 publications.

Numerous honours were bestowed on the outrider of astronomy. Johann Gottfried Herder dedicated his poem "Orion" to him. In 1802, he even was elevated to the hereditary peerage. But Hahn's greatest distinction was surely the naming of a moon crater on the northeast edge of the satellite after the adoptive Mecklenburger.

After Friedrich von Hahn's death in 1805, the observatory was no longer used for its primary purpose. The main building was pulled down in 1847. The tower of the oldest attestable observatory in Mecklenburg, which has been renovated by a team from the Archenhold Observatory in Berlin, still survives today.

Internet tip:
www.molau.de/remplin/rempline.html

Chronology of events

End of the Vistula Ice Age: hills, lakes and rivers developed — 10th millennium B.C.

Stone Age settlements emerged in the area of present day Mecklenburg-Western Pomerania — From the 8th millennium B.C.

The people of the Funnel Beaker Culture erected megalithic graves — 4th and 3rd millennium B.C.

Migration of peoples - Germanic tribes left the area Mecklenburg-Western Pomerania
Slavic peoples immigrated — 4th century A D till 6th century A.D.

First mention of the Slavic "Michelenburg" in present day Dorf Mecklenburg — 995

First use of the name "Pommern" in the chronicle "Annales Altahenses" — 1046

Henry the Lion defeated the Slavic prince Niklot / Founding of the town of Schwerin — 1160

The Pomeranian dukes Kasimir I and Bogislaw I became vassals of Henry the Lion — 1164

Pribislaw, son of Niklot, was enfeoffed with Mecklenburg — 1167

Bogislaw I received Pomerania from the German emperor Friedrich I — 1181

First major division of the state into four principalities (Mecklenburg, Rostock, Parchim-Richenberg, Werle-Güstrow) — 1229/35

13th century	Wismar, Rostock, Stralsund, Greifswald, Demmin, Anklam became Hanseatic Cities
1325	The Island of Rügen fell to Pomerania
1348	Karl IV made the Mecklenburg princes Albrecht II and Johann I imperial princes and conferred on them the title of duke
1370	Peace of Stralsund – King Waldemar IV of Denmark acknowledged the power of Hanseatic Cities in the Baltic Sea area
1419	Founding of the University of Rostock
1456	Founding of the University of Greifswald
1549	Sternberger Landtag (special council in Sternberg): proclamation of the Lutheran Faith to be the religion of the state
1618-1648	Thirty Years' War
1621	Second major division of the state (Mecklenburg-Schwerin and Mecklenburg-Güstrow)
1628	The emperor's commander Wallenstein became duke of both parts of the state
1648	The Peace of Westphalia: Wismar, Poel, the district of Neukloster and parts of Pomerania became part of Sweden
1654	Master-servant relationships established based on serfdom

Abolition of the Edict of Nantes: French Huguenots emigrated and settled in Bützow from 1703 onwards	1685
Third major division of the state into the dukedoms of Mecklenburg-Schwerin and Mecklenburg-Strelitz	1701
The Peace of Stockholm – Prussia received those parts of Western Pomerania from Sweden that lie south of the Peene and Usedom	1720
Ludwigslust was capital of the duchy Mecklenburg-Schwerin	1764
Abolition of torture in Mecklenburg	1769
Landed gentry demanded equality with the aristocracy at federal parliaments	1793
Pledge agreement with Sweden that returned Wismar to Mecklenburg	1803
French occupation of Mecklenburg and Pomerania	1806-1813
Queen Louise of Prussia died at Hohenzieritz castle	1810
Wars of Liberation against Napoleon	1813-1815
Congress of Vienna – Mecklenburg-Schwerin and Mecklenburg-Strelitz became grand dukedoms Prussia received Swedish part of Pomerania	1815

1820	Beginning of the abolition of serfdom
1848/1849	Election of a constituent assembly and adoption of a civil democratic constitution
1850	Arbitrament of Freienwalde – dissolution of the parliament and repeal of the constitution
1871	Grand dukedoms of Mecklenburg became federal states in the newly founded German Empire
1903	The city of Wismar, the island of Poel and the district of Neukloster belonged to Mecklenburg again
1918	November Revolution: Abdication of the grand dukes of Mecklenburg-Schwerin and Mecklenburg-Strelitz and of the Prussian king
1932	Election victory for the NSDAP in Mecklenburg-Schwerin and formation of a government, coalition government of German Nationalists and NSDAP in Mecklenburg-Strelitz
1934	Union of the free states of Mecklenburg-Schwerin and Mecklenburg-Strelitz
1939-1945	Second World War Establishment of detention camps and concentration camps for the arm industry
from 1942 on	Deportation of Jews from Mecklenburg and Prussian Pomerania
1945	Occupation of Mecklenburg by Soviet, British, Canadian, and American troops

Potsdam Conference separates Pomerania between Poland and Germany	1945
Founding of the Federal State of Mecklenburg-Western Pomerania	
Expropriation of industrial firms, land reform	
Elections held for the federal parliament of Mecklenburg-Western Pomerania resulting in a slight majority for the SED	1946
Upon Soviet orders, the name of Western Pomerania, „Vorpommern", was removed from the usual description of the federal state of Mecklenburg-Western Pomerania	1947
Dissolution of the state of Mecklenburg and creation of the municipalities of Neubrandenburg, Rostock and Schwerin	1952
"Action Rose": Expropriation of boarding houses and hotels along the Baltic Sea coast	1953
Closure of the Western border	1961
Establishment and modernisation of industrial companies in order to improve the infrastructure in the north of the GDR	from 1971 on
The German Turnaround and peaceful revolution, opening of the border to the Federal Republic of Germany	1989
German reunification Founding of the state of Mecklenburg-Western Pomerania, Schwerin became its capital	1990

1992 Start of the construction of the A 20 autobahn between Lübeck and Szczecin

2002 Historic centres of Wismar and Stralsund were together added to the UNESCO list of World Heritage Sites

2007 Mecklenburg-Western Pomerania was host to the G8 summit

Stammbaum der mecklenburgischen Fürsten.

Niklot † 1160[1].

Pribislaw 1167—78.

Heinrich Burwy I. 1179—1227[2].

(Heinrich Burwy II.)

Johann 1227—64, Herr zu Mecklenburg (Hauptlinie).	Nikolaus, Fürst zu Wenden. (Werle-Güstrow.) (Linie erlischt 1436.)	Heinrich Burwy III., Herr zu Rostock. (Linie erlischt 1314.)	Pribislaw † 1272, Herr zu Parchim. (Das Land fällt schon vor seinem Tode um 1256 an die anderen Linien.)
Heinrich I. der Pilger, 1264—1302.			
Heinrich II. der Löwe 1302—29.			

Albrecht II. der Große, Herzog von Mecklenburg 1329—79. Johann, Herzog von Stargard[3]. (Linie erlischt 1471 mit Herzog Ulrich.)

Heinrich III. 1379—84.	Albrecht III. 1379—1412[4].	Magnus I. 1379—84[5].	
Albrecht IV. † 1388.	Albrecht V. 1417—23.	Johann IV. 1395—1422.	Johanns Witwe Katharina Regentin 1423—86. Johann V. † 1443. Heinrichs IV. Sohn, Albrecht VI., † 1483.
		Heinrich IV. der Dicke 1436—77.	
		Magnus II. 1477—1503.	

Heinrich V. der Friedfertige 1503—52.   Albrecht VII. 1503—47.

Johann Albrecht I. 1547—76.   Ulrich 1555—1603.   Karl 1603—10[6].

Johann VII. 1585—92.

Adolf Friedrich I. von Mecklenburg-Schwerin 1592—1658.   Johann Albrecht II. von Mecklenburg-Güstrow 1611—36[7]. (Linie erlischt 1695 mit Gustav Adolf.)

Christian I. (Louis) 1658—92.   (Friedrich.)   Adolf Friedrich II. von Mecklenburg-Strelitz[8] 1701—08.

Friedrich Wilhelm, 1692—1713.   Karl Leopold 1713—47.   Christian II. Ludwig 1747—56.   Adolf Friedrich III. 1708—52.   (Karl Ludwig Friedrich.)

Friedrich der Fromme 1756—85.   (Ludwig.)   Adolf Friedrich IV. 1752—94.   Karl II., Großherzog 1794—1816.

Friedrich Franz I., Großherzog 1785—1837.   Georg 1816—60[9].

Friedrich Ludwig.

Paul Friedrich 1837—42.   Friedrich Wilhelm 1860—1904.

Friedrich Franz II. 1842—83.   Adolf Friedrich V. seit 1904 Gem.: Elisabeth von Adolf Friedrich[12]. Anhalt.

Friedrich Franz III.[10].   Johann Albrecht, 1883—97.   Regent 1897—1901.
Friedrich Franz IV. seit 1897 (1901)[11].
Gem.: Alexandra v. Cumberland.
Friedrich Franz geb. 1910.

Genealogical tree of the Dukes of Mecklenburg, from: Vitense, Otto. Mecklenburgische Geschichte. Berlin and Leipzig 1912.

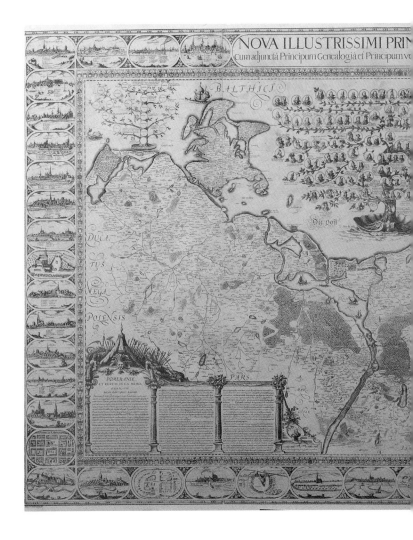

The Lubin Map not only depicts the genealogical tree of the dynasty, but also the history, the geography and the economic structure of Pomerania.

Picture Credits

Cover: Chalk cliffs on the island of Rügen, photograph by Thomas Grundner, Heiligendamm, photomontage by WERK3, Rostock

p. 11: Bundesbildstelle, Berlin; p. 13: Bert Aschkowski, Rostock; p. 14: Friederike Neubert, Zehna; p. 16: Handwerkskammer Schwerin; p. 17 and 18: AB Göta kanalbolag, Motala; p. 20: Freunde der Sabaki-Schule e. V., Rostock; p. 23: Österreichische Nationalbibliothek Wien; p. 25: Tourismusverband Mecklenburg-Vorpommern, Rostock (TMV); p. 27: Otto-Lilienthal-Museum, Anklam; p. 29: nordlicht, Rostock; p. 31: Thomas Grundner, Heiligendamm; p. 32: Zeitungsverlag Schwerin (ZVS); p. 34: Fritz-Reuter-Literaturmuseum, Stavenhagen; p. 37 and 39: ZVS; p. 40: Archiv der Hansestadt Stralsund; p. 42: Museen der Stadt Wolgast; p. 44: Maya Löffler, Hiddensee; p. 45: Peene Werft GmbH, Wolgast; p. 47: Charlotte Douglas International Airport; p. 48 (2): Hansa Soccer Academy, Chicago; p. 49: Town of Pomerode; 53: Stadt Ribnitz-Damgarten © VG Bild-Kunst, Bonn 2008; p. 54: Ateneum Art Museum, Helsinki / © The Munch Museum / The Munch Ellingsen Group / VG Bild-Kunst, Bonn 2008; p. 57 and 59: Stadt Sassnitz; p. 61: picture-alliance / dpa; p. 62: ZVS; p. 63: picture-alliance / dpa; p. 64: Fährhafen Sassnitz; p. 66, 67, 69 and 71: ZVS; p. 72: TMV; p. 75: © Renate von Mangoldt (Literarisches Colloquium Berlin); p. 76: Stefan Ziemendorff, Greifswald; p. 78: Andreas Nielsen, Wismar; p. 80: Mecklenburger Metallguss GmbH, Waren; p. 81: ZVS; p. 83: TMV; p. 84: Förderverein Jagdschloss Gelbensande e. V.; p. 87: multi-tech gGmbH, Dresden; p. 89: Stadt Bergen; p. 90: Hinstorff Verlag, Rostock; p. 93: TMV; p. 94: Thomas Grundner, Heiligendamm; p. 97: Deutsches Museum, München; p. 99 and 100: Technisches Museum Wien; p. 101: Esperanto-Zentrum, Dresden; p. 105: Schliemann-Museum, Ankershagen; p. 107: Archiv der Hansestadt Stralsund; p. 109 and 111: ZVS; p. 113: Archiv der Hansestadt Wismar; p. 115: Enrico Eisert / Hinstorff Media, Rostock; p. 116: © Hans-Werner Hausmann, Universität Greifswald; p. 118: Claudia Haiplick, Löbnitz; p. 120: Jana Sperber, Rostock; p. 121: Andreas Bartelmann, Kühlungsborn-West; p. 123: Karstadt Warenhaus GmbH, Filiale Wismar; p. 127: TMV; p. 129: Voith Turbo Scharfenberg GmbH & Co. KG, Salzgitter; p. 130: Peter Falow, Radegast; p. 131: picture-alliance / dpa; p. 133 and 135: ZVS; p. 137: Museum Oskar Reinhart am Stadtgarten, Winterthur; p. 139: TMV; p. 143: W. Sauer Orgelbau Frankfurt (Oder) GmbH; p. 146: Thomas Grundner, Heiligendamm; p. 149 and 150: Quick Maritim Medien, Rechlin; p. 152 and 155: TMV; p. 156 and 157: Müritzeum gGmbH; 159: ZVS; p. 160: TMV; p. 161 and 164: ZVS; p. 166: Flughafen Rostock-Laage-Güstrow GmbH; p. 168: Hinstorff Verlag, Rostock; p. 170: TMV; p. 172 and 174: Hans-Heinrich Schimler, Rostock; p. 177, 179 and 180: ZVS; p. 181: Universität Rostock; p. 183: Deutsches Meeresmuseum, Stralsund; p. 185: Carsten Pescht, Rostock; p. 186 and 187: Schlosshotel Gutshaus Ludorf; p. 188: Hinstorff Verlag, Rostock; p. 191: © Markus Möller / Ronald Prokein, Rostock; p. 194 and 195: Gerhard H. Ehlers, Odenthal; p. 197: TMV; p. 206/7: Pommersches Landesmuseum, Greifswald.

We would like to sincerely thank all who contributed to this publication. Author, editors and publishing house attempted to identify owners of copyright and to index them correctly. In the event that any details identified as not wholly correct, the editor would welcome any comments in order to make amendments.